Lighten Up

by Linda J. Martin

To : Amber,
Thank you so much
for caring. My
wrist is better
already.
Enjoy my book!
With love,
Linda

Lighten Up . . . Diets Don't Work YOU Do

paperback edition 978-1-62122-003-9
ePub 978-1-62122-004-6
pdf 978-1-62122-005-3
Mobi 978-1-62122-006-0
exeBook 978-1-62122-007-7
Multiple eBook Formats on CD 978-1-62122-008-4

Library of Congress Cataloging-in-Publication Data

Martin, Linda, 1943-
.Lighten up, diets don't work you do / by Linda Martin. -- Paperback edition
pages cm   ISBN 978-1-62122-003-9 (paperback) – ISBN 978-1-62122-
004-6 (ePub ebook) -- ISBN 978-1-62122-005-3 (pdf eBook) -- ISBN 978-
1-62122-006-0 (mobi eBook) -- ISBN 978-1-62122-007-7 (exeBook eBook)
1. Weight loss--Psychological aspects. 2. Food--Psychological aspects. 3.
Mind and body. I. Title.   RM222.2.M3657 2012

                                                            _ 613.2'5--dc23.

2012022875

Credits
Graphic Design: Designs by Stephanie, MOI Books
Cover Design: Bob Maus

CONTENTS

PART IV
THE EMOTIONAL

PART V
THE SPIRITUAL

Lighten Up is dedicated to YOU.

ACKOWLEDGEMENTS

Sometimes in life you wonder how you arrived at a certain place. This is a time in my life that I'm filled with deep gratitude for all the wonderful people who have made this creative project come to a close. Over the years, I've received the care and love of many teachers, therapists, healers and mentors who have brought me to a place that I now have something to express. It was not by my efforts alone that I am able to write these words.

Thank you Franchesca, my talented and gifted mother for you were the first to plant the seed, the idea to write a book. I know you've been with me throughout this project, whispering in my ear. Thanking all my beloved Practitioner friends at the Rio Grande Center for Spiritual Living in Albuquerque, New Mexico for their support and prayers. To my wonderful editor, Teresa Cutler-Broyles who was there for me every moment and became my best cheerleader. We spent countless hours together and created a book that will give to others the precious gifts of healing as I've received. She convinced me my book had to be written. To my dear friend, John Meluso who filled my days with support and encouragement. Because of his patience and listening, I became a better person and communicator. To my beautiful and beloved Aunt Princine who encouraged me to write and never give up. Her words of inspiration kept me motivated.

To my friends and family, thank you so much for listening to me over the years talk incessantly about the writing of my book. You were so patient and I appreciate your encouragement. To all my wonderful contributors who took the time and effort to write healing words, and present techniques to help us live our lives in the most positive, productive, and uplifting ways. My dear friend and teacher, Reverend Jesse Jennings, founder of the Creative Life Spiritual Center in Spring, Texas who gave us a wonderful explanation of affirmative prayer, a tool we can use to begin to change our lives. Saundra Dickinson, who through her healing efforts brought me into a new way of listening and being. Her contributions of Imago Therapy and EMDR help us move beyond our fears and the past. Beverly Nadler, my friend, teacher and healer who was so generous in giving us information on a powerful healing modality, Emotional Freedom Technique. EFT has helped me uncover beliefs that kept me stuck in many areas in my life. Bill Ferguson, thank you for helping me to heal past wounds and to know I have a right to be here. You are passing on your healing technique to help others heal and making a difference in the world. Dell Deberadinis, my precious friend and brilliant therapist who makes me laugh through the thick and thin of it all. I'm in awe of your brilliance and thank you for making a difference in the lives of those who suffer. Reverend Martha Quintana, minister of the Rio Grande Center for Spiritual Living, my friend and mentor who helps me remember who I am. May the blessings of Spirit fill your hearts and lives to the fullest. In deep gratitude, I thank you.

INTRODUCTION

❥

ACCORDING TO The American Obesity Association, 64% of the U.S. population is overweight or obese. If diet products worked, wouldn't you think this number would be lower? How many of us have flocked to diets promising weight loss, happiness, a life free of shame and guilt, then try another diet when the first doesn't work. Or the second. Or the third.

What if diets weren't the answer? What if you could begin to live your life from this moment forward free of diets, free of shame, free of guilt? Would you believe a person who overcame the battle of the bulge and answered yes to the questions above? Believe it, that's me!

Do you feel your life is hectic, pathetic and out of control with food, constantly dieting and bingeing? Do you feel out of control with many things in your life? I dieted and binged my way through high school and college, and on into my first doomed marriage. Do you have a similar story, filled with pain, guilt, and self-hate? Stories change.

My life is different now and yours will be also. If you're reading this information, you're ready to begin the journey that guarantees a life of happiness. Living comfortably with yourself, and never using food to try to fix the hidden reasons that once drove you unconsciously to the refrigerator, will be your new experiences. You will eat what you want and when you want without any thought of dieting. I've found the **SECRETS** *to the doorway of success and will share every one of them with you.* They've helped me maintain my weight for over thirty years. You will live in gratitude and awe instead of obsessing over your weight and food issues. This can be our story. You are headed for an unprecedented life.

Many people have overcome food issues and the insanity of dieting. There are many paths. The path I offer you is very different and will open you up to a new way of seeing and living your life, and a way out of your private fears. As you most likely know, many diet books talk about food values, calories, grams of fat, and carb content. In these things, most of us who have struggled with food issues are experts. Are you a diet expert? I was and knew every diet in vogue, every calorie in a banana and chocolate bar, every carbohydrate gram in a slice of bread and an apple.

Although we have all this information committed to memory, it is of no value whatsoever. I still dieted and binged and was out of control, and I continued to live my life overweight and in constant crisis. I'm no longer a diet expert. Do you want to be a diet expert or do you want to resolve all your food issues? I know it's the latter.

Many diet books are filled with recipes and suggested menus, and you probably have some of them. This book includes some of those tools but discovering how to have a healthy relationship with food and with yourself is much more important than recipes and menus. Many different tools and techniques will be revealed for the first time, tools that you can immediately implement in your daily life.

Food issues extend into many areas of life, and food may only be the physical manifestation of those other issues, the most visible one. Food can be a Band-Aid, covering up everything we're afraid to face, or feel. My life was a living hell, and Band-Aids didn't help but I had no other tools. Do you want to remove the Band-aids? With your commitment, it's certain to be different. I promise.

Lighten Up is bigger, much bigger than resolving food issues. It is about the Power that lies within all of us that moves us forward.

Since you picked up this book, I know a core of hope exists and that's all it takes to begin this journey. With this sliver of hope, we are creating a healthy foundation for the new you. Something inside you is calling you to rally on. Your gifts and talents are screaming to emerge and the best part is you're now in the process of letting things go that no longer serve you. This allows you freedom to get in touch with your gifts and to act upon them. Your experiences and personal growth will be different from mine, and as you move toward the you you will become, tell me what your discoveries are.

Send me your stories. Tell me what worked.

Visit my blog: www.DietsDontWorkYouDo.com.

I will be sharing many of my personal stories with you.

www.DietsDontWorkYouDo.com/PersonalStories.html

Our Physical, Mental, Emotional and Spiritual bodies comprise our total being. Each one will be addressed individually and you will clearly understand the effects food issues have on our health and well being. Before you know it, the positive changes you are making in your life will become permanent, comfortable patterns.

Throughout this book, you will be hearing from other experts in the field of healing and recovery. Included are an Imago Therapist, a Sexual Abuse Therapist, an ex-attorney who gave up his practice to help others, and an Emotional Freedom Technique expert, to assist you along the path of many changes. I can assure you much of the information is fresh and finally available.

My wish for you is that you will be free in ways you've never imagined. You are about to discover that food is not your problem and that's your first giant leap to freedom. Expect surprises around every corner.

Be patient, have faith, finding success is certain. Courage grows self-confidence. Faith replaces fear. Willingness to become open to change builds a Spiritual strength beyond understanding.

This takes time, and true desire to look deeply within and a realization that you will be afraid, that you will be vulnerable, and that you will, you will reach a place where you no longer are in agony over food issues, your weight, or body image.

Take hold of the positive and keep it by your side. When it starts to stray, and it will pull it back with the next best positive thought. You are creating a new you. Be fearless.

PART I

WHERE FOOD OBSESSION TOOK ME

Darkness is lifeless and powerless

♥

CHAPTER 1

An Addictive Life

WHAT FOLLOWS WILL GIVE YOU AN IDEA of how I lived and what I thought of myself. The compulsions, the overeating, the obsession with food got in my way of love, creativity, happiness, peace, and all the good that life has to offer. I didn't know I was destined for greatness but I know now. I acknowledge your greatness and now you're in flight. We are all in each others' hearts.

I obsessed daily, moment by moment, about food, eating it, buying it, hiding it, planning it, preparing it, and spending a fortune on it. I was driven to have that fix. Food was more important than anything else: people, places, things. One bite was too much and one hundred bites were not enough. I ate and ate until I couldn't take another bite, and yet I ate more. My stomach hurt and I continued to eat. I couldn't zip my pants and I continued to eat. I couldn't stop. Day after day, year after year, the insanity had a life all of its own. I was burning in hell and I was alive. I constantly dreamed about being thin. That was my number one goal in life, really the only goal. I thought if I was thin, I would be liked, noticed and accepted. I would be loved. If I was thin, I would be happy and all my problems would be solved. Being thin was the answer to all my problems. I played those tapes over and over.

I laughed and smiled a lot; I was masking my excruciating pain and faking it all. The truth is I didn't have a voice that was mine. The world dictated my voice.

My heart was pounding much of the time, not because I was proud of my accomplishments but because my sugar level was sky high. My heart felt as if it would burst because it was beating so fast. I was afraid of most things: failure, success, both. Relationships were difficult, with both people and money. I had no relationship with myself. Dreams faded into nothing. I believed I was a failure in many aspects of my life. I was afraid of life. I had so life.

I hated how I looked. I was never satisfied with myself. I was my worst critic. The criticism in my head was constant. Everyone was better than I. Everyone was smarter, more successful, more everything. How could anyone really like me, or see me as valuable? I put everyone else and their needs first. Others' feelings and happiness were more important than mine. Being the peacemaker was high on my priority list. I didn't consider myself worthy of being on any list. I didn't think I had any creative ideas of my own.

I did, however, have deep feelings. I just didn't know how to express any of them, good or bad. So I stuffed all the feelings and thoughts down inside with food. Food was my greatest friend in times of need. Food was my substitute for all the things in life I wanted and didn't have.

I was passionate about food. It was my high, my happiness. I was comforted by it. The taste that satisfied me deeply gave me a false sense that all was well. I would move mountains to get to my favorite food. I often left my warm bed in the middle of the night to satisfy my insatiable craving for sweets or carbs or salty chips, frantically trying to satisfy my desperate need for chocolate. I had no control over the cravings.

I envied people who could eat a cookie and be completely satisfied. "Why can't I be like that," I asked? I felt I had been cursed. "Why me?"

Every Monday was the day that everything was going to be different. My diet began sharply at 9:00 am. I told myself it would be different this go around. My enthusiasm was high. Determination was my middle name.

Monday was easy. I skipped breakfast and rushed to work. I had my usual diet lunch, a green salad piled high with veggies, no salad dressing only vinegar. A little tangy but I downed it. Dinner came and went. I wasn't too hungry. I got home late and it was almost bedtime. I ate that apple in front of the TV. One minute it was there and the next it was gone. What happened to it? Where did the core go? Eager for the next day, I felt great. I was in control today. Thinking tomorrow would be just as easy, I fell asleep.

The week went well. However, when Friday came I just couldn't help rewarding myself with snacks at the open bar. Just a few. I rationalized that I was strong during the week. I said no to the goodies at work. I said no to my friends who asked me to go for lunch. I exercised each day, sometimes twice. I weighed myself daily, many times during the day to see how I was doing. Surely I could have a few snacks without a problem one day a week. So I did. Great, all was well. I was in control.

Then I went home to an empty house or one filled with people, but empty nonetheless, was when something shifted. Before I realized it, as if some force had taken control of my being, I would shove cookies into my mouth, faster and faster. I couldn't get them down fast enough. And it felt so good. The taste and the feelings were all-powerful. Suddenly, no more cookies. I still had some ice cream from last week. Almost tripping over my feet, I ran to the freezer. The ice cream was gone, but it was before midnight and I knew the convenience store was still open. Speeding like a mad person, rounding the last bend, I saw the store owner pull away. How could he leave at a time like this?

The night was still and dark as I drove home in quiet desperation. I was numb, and I felt as if I was the last person on earth. An empty person fell into an empty bed. I lay very still, my heart pounding. I didn't know what the feeling was but today I know it was terror. I repeated my mantra, "I must stay on my diet. I know I can do it. I'll try harder." My eyes closed, full of tears.

Saturday. I awake hating myself. The house is quiet. Some would say peaceful but not me, not this morning. Quiet and loneliness are too closely connected. My anxiety level is high, my stomach hurts from last night's binge. It is difficult to go to the bathroom. Guilt and shame clothe my being, and the crazy voices run through my mind, yapping like a dog chained to a tree.

"How could I do that again? I am so stupid. I can't do anything. I'll never lose the weight. What's wrong with me?" I ask. Looking in the mirror I see only ugliness and disgust. How could anyone love me? I'll hide. No one must know my secret, my many secrets.

One of my secrets was that I obsessed over diets pills; this morning I promised myself no more pills but I always had some if I needed that extra help. It was difficult to endure the side effects, however it did give me confidence knowing I had them. For over five years during my college days, I was a pill-popping freak. I didn't know I had a problem. Hell's hot.

Yet, it was a new day, a new beginning of a mindless, hopeless day. The sun was glorious, but I knew how it would play out. I felt all my confidence slip away, all the control I had during the week was gone. The switch had been turned on and I was in another zone. Food was almighty. It was my best friend, and I hid in its comfort. It gave me a feeling of safety. It was my life. No one could take it away from me. Nothing nor anyone was more important than my love for food. It was my solace, my happiness, and my greatest love. It gave me everything I could ever want or need, so I thought. The *Food Lover* had me. I was being seduced. I was trapped in the arms of insanity once again. I was fighting for my life.

I loved the food. I hated the food. I hated myself. Contradictions. And I continued to eat. As I ate, the tears streamed down my face and I wanted to stop. I was full. I couldn't have been hungry! Wondering where the food was going, I ate more and more; faster and faster like a machine out of control. I was battling with the enemy. Who will win? My thoughts were foggy. Who am I? Where am I? What am I doing? There was no light anywhere, only darkness. I felt crazy. I was crazy. I knew what insanity was. "Stop it, stop it, stop it," I screamed, but I couldn't.

"Someone help me. Is there anyone there?" I didn't have many friends. I didn't know what I thought about people. Today I look back and know I was afraid. When I was with people, I was often criticized. They would say things like: "Where are you putting all that food?" "You're going to eat the entire cake, if you aren't careful." "You're going to explode." The criticism made me want to eat more, so I did. What few friends I did have, I believed they took advantage of me. I only wanted to help them. I always seemed to know what they needed and when. I felt I knew what was best and told them quite often, without considering if they were asking for help. I had a desire to fix people and situations. I offended people. I was unaware. I took things personally. I cried easily.

And I stuffed the feelings of hurt, isolation and insecurity deeper into the pit of no return. Eating was my great companion. Who really needed anyone anyway? Another lost day. Full of self-pity, I turned out the light.

Sunday was my day of rationalization but it would be more honest to call it a day of self-slaughter. It was the last day of the weekend, and finally I could *lighten up*. Again, Monday was a new beginning. Almost in relief, I planned to give myself one more day of eating, because tomorrow, Monday my diet day, I would begin the cycle again. Sunday, I could eat all day long. Pleasure, yum yum. I could get in as much and as often as I wanted. I cleaned out the cabinets so the temptation would not be there. I was happy to find the chocolate sauce, just enough for two pints of ice cream. Off to the store I went, and on the way I decided to buy cookies to go with the ice cream. I was happy, anticipating both my fix and the next day's new beginning. I would appear happy to anyone who crossed my path with my smiles, my laughter, the mask.

Beneath the anticipation of the ice cream, and the new diet, I was screaming. I wasn't sure what for, but the deepest part of me knew the ice cream wasn't it. The cookies, ice cream, and a bag of chips filled my car and I raced home. Honestly, I could never wait until I get home. My busy little hands ripped open the bag, cookies flew over the seat onto the floor. It didn't matter; I ate them anyway, dirt and all.

I ran into the kitchen tripping over my feet, looking for a clean spoon. Hurry. Hurry. Hurry. The sink was usually lined with dirty dishes and silverware. Nothing clean. The desire to eat was always greater than cleanliness. It didn't matter if they were dirty. There was time to clean up later. That wasn't important. Nothing mattered then. Nothing. Ice cream in a dirty bowl, a dirty spoon to eat it with, that was monumentally important.

Into my mouth and directly into my veins it went. *Ahhhhhhhh* that warm, calm feeling again, that welcome glow from head to toe. Suddenly, my body was in a different place. Food was my drug, my fix and it was kicking in. Cocaine into my veins. I ate myself into a stupor, my thoughts were hazy. But I was aware of how good it all felt, and how hopeless, powerless and helpless I was. I hated every part of my being, but I loved the warmth, the love, that powerful feeling of control. Those insane contradictions again. I rationalized again. Tomorrow was a new day and I would begin again, stronger than before.

Sunday night. I had been eating all weekend. Job well done! The cabinets were pretty clean. A few handfuls of lettuce, a bag of carrots. I was ready for tomorrow. I was uncomfortable. I had to unbutton my pants for the last few hours. It was time to put on my robe. I could move better. My stomach hurt and my skin stretched across my body like a tight rubber band. I wondered what overeating was doing to me physically, how it affected my heart, my skin, my every-thing. I panicked. I ate more.

The last thing I would do on those Sunday nights would be to jump on the scale. That way I would be clear about how much weight I wanted to lose during the week. It was part of the ritual. The scale and I played a game. I hated that scale. It talked back to me. It mirrored the deepest part of my soul. My record for hopping on and off the scale in one hour was ten times. I counted. My thought was have I gained or lost any weight in an hour? It wasn't uncommon for me to gain five pounds over the weekend. The scale lies, I thought. I kicked it. I thought it was broken. I would go to my backup scale. Five pounds! In three days. I was horrified. Then again, it wasn't as bad as some of the other times when it was almost eight pounds in four days. I would starve myself for five days after that, and those eight pounds came off. I always knew I could do that again. I believed I was strong, I could do anything. I took a deep breath, telling myself, Monday at 9:00 am would be another new beginning and by Friday, I could drop those unwanted pounds. I was busy going nowhere fast. Year after year after year. Stories change.

CHAPTER 2

A Miraculous Life

OVER THE YEARS since that time, people have often asked me how did I stay so slim and eat so much. Hum, how did I do that? I wondered myself. It just happened or did it? Then, during the spring of 2006, a soft voice whispered in my ear: "Do it, Do it." What was it? I had no idea, but I found myself writing and soon I was blasted out of my comfort zone. Something compelled me to put together this book of healing information to help others who suffered as I did. I thought it would be a simple recounting of my journey. Silly me.

I had no idea how emotionally and mentally humbling the writing of this book would be. I found it difficult to reveal my bizarre behavior. I felt vulnerable and exposed much of the time, naked. I didn't want you to know the depths to which I had sunk, the despair I once felt. Wacky stuff, like eating food out of the garbage. Eek! Sometimes we have to put ourselves out there and expose ourselves to help others. Would you be willing to share your failures and, soon, your successes? If your story is anything like mine, and if my story brings you the opportunity to shift into a new way of living, as I have, then I have fulfilled my purpose. I have a deep desire to be of service. Perhaps one day your story will be told.

I'm so different now. This is the new me and this is how I live, and this is what I wanted people to know about me. As I dove into the past and into the journey that got me here, I realized my past is part of what makes me who I am.

Today, I don't do any of the bizarre behavior I once did, ever. As you read **Lighten Up,** you'll see the turning points which steered me in different directions; putting the diet pill sage to rest, having my last bite of chocolate, the Spiritual awakening, the most profound. Change didn't happen overnight. Many changes occurred over a period of time. You'll discover more of the experiences I encountered during those years and I'll bring you up to date with lots of good in the present.

Here is a taste of what heaven looks and feels like in my world today. I wanted to share lots of successes with the thought you can have a similar story, even better.

I now live in a new reality after waking up from a horrible nightmare. I remember the nightmare, and now I revel in the present and anticipate the future. I am out of hell. I am excited about the future, mine and yours. It has to do with living our passion, our dreams, about the talents and gifts we all have.

What are your passions, your dreams? Have you forgotten or viewed them as impossible? They aren't impossible. You have desires that are unique to you. Desires have been placed inside all of us, like whispers nudging us forward. Deep down we know but somehow we're afraid, not trusting, sometimes stuffing our feelings down with food. "Who am I to think I could accomplish great things." You have a right to think and be who you want. You will learn to accept your goodness. I continue to accept mine with gratitude.

I have a play in the making after this book is published. It compliments the book. It is about you and me. Living my passion is thrilling. We're here to do good, be good and have good. When I was in the throes of food issues, writing the book and creating my play would never have popped into my consciousness.

View a selection from my solo perfomance, *The Gift*.

www.DietsDontWorkYouDo.com/dance.html

There's more. You know how a baby suddenly finds its hand and is mesmerized by it, looking around in utter amazement? That's how it is with me. I walk around daily in awe over the magic and mystery of this thing called life. I am at peace. This is pure happiness. Everything is from the inside out. I got it. "**SECRETS,** *To losing weight from the inside out.*"

I walk on solid ground. There is a foundation under my feet supporting me with every step I take. Faith has replaced fear, fear of people and fear of success. My heart is open, loving my days and loving the wonderful people in my life. With great anticipation, I look forward to all my new friends, including you. I have accomplished much and I dream big. Serenity is now my middle name. Imagine, what is your middle name?

At times, I'm challenged by situations. Sometimes life isn't easy but I understand that's life. I now have tools and resources available to put into action to help during the difficult times. They will pass. Sometimes not quick enough! I have courage to ask for help and to ask for what I need. I'm aware when it's time to let things go and I sometimes have to remind myself to let them go. I do my best and I appreciate who I am. Before you read another word, put this book down, put your arms around yourself, give yourself a big hug and say, "Wonderful, Wonderful, Wonderful Me." You are Wonderful just because you are you.

I live knowing I'm at choice. I'm at choice to love myself or beat myself up. I choose love. I've learned love is all there is. More on the love topic later.

As I'm writing, I realize I've not mentioned food. Interesting. Food is not my problem. It never was. Well, what about the food? I still love food, and my friends and family will attest to that. I love to eat it, love to buy it, love to prepare it. When I'm finished eating, I'm finished. The body says stop and I stop. There is never any inner debate. I know I weigh the same because my clothes fit year after year. I don't own a scale. I haven't thought about dieting for so long it's difficult to remember. That's freedom.

Connection with God, excellent radiant health, freedom from food issues, living my passion and love are the greatest gifts, in my humble opinion. Everything else is icing on the cake!

I've paved the way for seekers and now it will be easier for those who desire freedom from food issues. I believe it was suppose to be this way. There was a purpose. I think you'll understand when you read the information in the Spiritual section.

It seems like a life time ago I was in hell. Maybe several lifetimes ago. I've morphed into many different characters along the way. Think about it, you are a different person than you were a year ago. Much different than two or five years ago. Shocking if you go back even further. Who were you? Who are you now? Who do you want to become?

This book is full of incredible information, processes, and tools to improve the quality of your life and I know your life will get better and better as mine did. Whether it's food issues, a behavior or a belief keeping your down, they will fall away. With help, faith and taking action, you can do anything. I will show you how to make amazing changes on many levels and move from a place that feels like paralysis, to one that is filled with freedom, joy, and unexpected miracles. You've made the commitment to be the best you can be. Congratulations.

PART II

THE PHYSICAL

A happy face is half the meal

❤

CHAPTER 3

Food and More

❤

"AT LEAST MY HABIT ISN'T COCAINE. It's just food." That sounds simple, doesn't it? But do you know a cocaine habit is easier to break than overcoming food issues? Are you surprised? We can let go of cocaine, alcohol and other addictions because we don't need them. We have to eat to live as food is our nourishment. No getting around this one. It's not been simple, has it?

We are conditioned. The thought of going to parties, celebrations, events, always made me smile. Good times and food go together. I fantasized about the display of food. I was more excited about the food than seeing the people who were attending the event. Salivating began when the invitation was opened.

And of course the holidays dictate what kind of foods we eat. Turkey for Thanksgiving and Christmas. The ham for Easter. Black eyed peas for New Years. Irish Stew for St. Patrick's Day. Do you begin thinking about the turkey dinner early in November? Writing about it makes me salivate and it's March! Holidays used to be a great excuse to gorge. Everything tasted so much better.

Our conditioning isn't our fault. Much of it is how we grew up in our culture. The whirl began early without our awareness. Our obsessions begin when we're young, and now we eat when we're happy, sad, lonely, tired, embarrassed, feeling less than. Plug in the emotion. In depth questions are a great way to begin the process of self-evaluation.

For your personal assessment of in depth questions:

www.DietsDontWorkYouDo.com/assessment.html

What I discovered was this: food was not the problem. My relationship to food was the problem, and my relationship to life. That insight was both a shock and a relief. Here are some startling statistics based in part on the Diagnostic and Statistical Manual, 4th Edition, of the American Psychiatric Association:

· *One in five people in the United States has an eating disorder.*
· *People who diet in their teens increase their chances of developing an eating disorder eightfold.*
· *Ninety-five percent of people who diet gain back their weight and often surpass their previous high weight.*

It is brutally clear that diets are not the problem but the relationship to food is the problem, not food. The relief came in knowing a relationship needed to be healed. The shock was it was not the food. Now I had hope. The hope took me deep inside and began to push me toward a new life. I hope you're feeling hopeful. Something is pushing you toward a new life.

"At least it wasn't cocaine." I affirm again, dealing with food issues is worse than overcoming a cocaine habit. There is no getting away from having to eat, of potentially being triggered to continue to eat until gaining five pounds in three days. Insanity.

Throughout this book I offer you many **SECRETS** which will take you to unexplored territories, gathering many gifts along the way. You'll discover how to overcome the insanity around food issues and how to turn that hell into heaven, daily.

Beginning to understand food is not the problem

Most of us deal with food issues based on our relationship with our bodies. We become our bodies. Are you dealing only with your physical body? If so, perhaps that is one of the reasons you haven't had the success you desperately desire. We're going to learn to deal with ourselves in different ways, and making changes in healthy ways that are permanent. You're going to discover things that are perfect for you and only you, making life easy in ways you've not experienced before.

Much of the Physical section deals with getting your food intake in order with meal planning, choosing healthy foods to eat, and many more guidelines. When you begin to find balance with your new food plan, eating well and feeling great, everything becomes easier. As you find the balance, you'll also have a more conscious recognition of the issues behind the food, which are leading to the challenges.

You are learning to eat to nourish your body, look and feel great, and have tremendous amounts of energy while feeling satisfied. You are developing a new mindset and your consciousness is changing.

Since our focus has been on the obsession with food, it may appear to be the biggest concern. But we know food isn't our problem. We have a gnawing awareness that something is behind our food issues but we ignore it instead of diving in and exploring it. And we hate it and all the pain it causes. Do you think we're afraid? Do you think there's something outside ourselves that would make a difference, make our lives better, help us heal? It is you who is making a profound difference.

Removing the shackles of diets and diet pills

You've probably tried every diet imaginable, and know what diets are in vogue at any given moment. The grapefruit diet, the diet-pill diet, the poodo diet, and the water diet were just a few I tried. They were all manifestations of my food obsession.

The water diet. For a moment, imagine walking in winter slush with your feet making that slushy noise. When I was on the water diet, every time I moved, turned or walked, my body made that same slushy noise. It was embarrassing. I felt I was carrying a swimming pool in my stomach. I'm certainly not opposed to drinking water, and indeed it is important to get enough. It makes sense to feed your body water, since the majority of our bodies are made of water. Yes, drink water. Stop short of the slushy, squishy noises.

I had to dig deep in my memory bank to remember why I was so enthralled over the water diet. It was suppose to make me feel full and cut down on the food I was consuming. I did feel full but I ate anyway. So much for that diet fad.

The diet-pill diet. This information is for diet pill poppers. Who in their right mind would take diet pills? That was me. I wasn't in my right mind. Those pills are like little bullets going off in your body, revving you up like that little energized bunny. They can't be good for us, and we know that. We'll try anything, won't we? When I was on that poison, I was like a energized bunny. I never stopped. I lay awake at night with dry cotton mouth and couldn't sleep. It all started when my mother gave me the pills during a semester break from college. She had taken them for years and felt they would be good for me. She must have thought I looked a little fluffy. Who could have known it would turn out to be the beginning of a tragic period in my life? Now in addition to being a food addict, I was a full blown, pill popping wreck; I had two addictions to deal with, with no clue what I was doing other than spinning my wheels and going nowhere fast. With the help of those pills, I dieted and binged for many lost years during my college career. I still wonder how I graduated. I was in a vicious diet and binge cycle with the toxic partnership of the diet pill high. All of it put me in a fog. My memory recall makes my mouth dry.

The poodo diet. I'll skip that one. *Purging,* can't go there either.

The diet pill frenzy. My food issues never took a break, vacation or a holiday. It didn't matter if I was in school or on summer break. I was always obsessing over food and my weight. There was nothing in between. I had no peace around food and always had a good supply of diet pills wherever I found myself.

Obsession and compulsion go together, like control and manipulation. During summer breaks, many college students went to the shore to wait tables. On the surface, they were hoping to earn money for school, but in reality the real intent was to party. I got a job waiting tables just like the rest of my friends and found that a restaurant was a great place to work if one has food issues. I learned to sneak food and lots of it. Binge and diet, diet and binge.

One fateful day I ran out of diet pills. I panicked. It felt as if I had no control at all. Although it happened many years ago, I remember the episode as if it were yesterday. I literally ran to every drug store in Wildwood, New Jersey, to see if I could get the prescription refilled. The date had expired and no one seemed to believe that if I didn't have the pills I was going to die! I was out of control, speeding, fueled by fear and desperation, and I felt as if I was out of my body watching my own crazy antics. Finally, one of the pharmacists phoned the infirmary at WVU and got them to refill the prescription over the phone. I left the drug store in heaven: thrilled, relieved, happy. Being thin was just around the corner, once more.

I didn't want to repeat that harried experience again so I devised a plan. First, I purchased some empty clear capsules. I then spread them out in front of me and sat for hours dividing up the little multi-colored beads. Light blue ones, pink ones, yellow ones, and white ones. I wondered if anyone else had ever been so meticulous. I counted the exact number of beads over and over again, and put them into their individual capsules. They were perfect. Success!

Life was good once more and I had hope, but did I? Was that insanity? Yes, it was; it was the height of pure neurotic behavior. I made a mess of things quite often. Now I make a mess sometimes. Great improvement. I remember my humanness. Have you tried diet pills? Do you take them or use any other kind of Band-Aids? If so, you'll be off of them soon.

I remember two things about that event most particularly, things which turned out to be turning points in my life, which I alluded to earlier. I can't really explain it. Perhaps an angel watched my antics and decided to give me a rest. I made my first conscious decision about changing my behavior. First, for a brief moment during all that racing around and separating teensy beads, I recognized what I was doing as insane. Second, somewhere during the sorting I made a conscious decision that I would never again take diet pills, and this was the last prescription I would ever, ever get. And it was. I weaned myself off of them slowly and it was both wonderful and terrible. Those little beads were priceless jewels and once they were gone they were gone forever.

That conscious thought did not turn into other conscious thoughts about food but it was the beginning. And while I was free from the addiction of diet pills, I was still in the dark for many years and my insanity around food was still there and of course got worse. Those were lonely days. Do you ever feel lonely? I remember visiting my friends in the dorm just to eat their care packages from home; I could hit the entire first floor in an hour. Susie had the chocolate chip cookies, and Jeannie had the fudge. What a vivid memory. Addiction grows wings and flies in many directions if not treated and I hadn't done a thing to treat it. I didn't know what the word addiction meant. It was just my life. I was on a roll.

However, there is always hope, and the world offers incredible ways to heal and unfold into the magnificent beings that we are. I didn't know anyone in those days who experienced the same insanity I was living. No one talked about food issues. Everyone seemed to eat and not have any concerns or problems, just me. I looked around and no one was doing the things I did. Maybe many lies were lived and I didn't recognize it. It was all about me. I really believed I was all alone on my own, in my own world. I had many secrets all bottled up inside. I could never admit them to anyone, not even to myself. Perhaps others hid their own secrets. I never considered that idea. Funny huh! The feeling of being alone was deep in my gut. The pain ripped me apart like a sharp razor blade cutting in many directions. There was no relief. I was never alone, but I didn't find that out until much later on my journey. Through my shared experiences, your miles will be shorter.

I'm here to truly help you. If you don't believe what I'm sharing, I understand, since my promises may seem unattainable. If you choose to follow these suggestions, you'll see great results. You will be a perfect test result. The most important thing is that you don't have to do it alone any longer or feel alone. The truth is you've never been alone, just like me. You'll see, if you already don't know.

The feelings of being out of control with food issues are truly becoming a thing of the past. From this moment on, pretend the word diet doesn't exist. It's such a negative word, isn't it? It sends shivers down my spine. Immediately, I think Monday morning, deprivation, starving, failure, self-hate, binge, weight gain, tight pants, fat thighs, and a fat butt. It goes on and on, and is contagious. Dieting is torture, physically and mentally. And now, diets are over, done, finished, not to be mentioned again. No more prescriptions for those little bullets either. It's time to live in freedom.

REMEMBER

*   Influence of Holidays
*   In depth questions
*   Statistics
*   Diets and diet pills

CHAPTER 4

Guidelines to Freedom with Food

❥

Eat to Lose

SECRET. *If you want to lose weight, you have to eat.* Starving is not the answer. Our bodies need fuel to run. If we don't eat enough, our bodies go into crisis mode, grabbing and storing fat. This is the perfect recipe to stay in Hell. In fact, starving sets us up for failure. If you deprive yourself all day, likely you'll sit down to a meal at night and consume the entire refrigerator. You know the results. Tomorrow will be another day of self-hate and on and on. So how do we change that? What is the new behavior? We're beginning to tread on new territory.

Choice

SECRET. *We are at choice in everything we think and feel.* We can decide at any given moment to change anything: behaviors, actions. Choose to eat sensibly. **SECRET.** *Learning to eat sensibly means discovering new eating habits and finding ways that work for you.* It becomes easy as you go along making positive choices and changes. You're doing it now without angst or problem. Yes, best to decide to eat sensibly. It becomes a joyful experience. What a ride you're in for. You're on a path toward an endless destination.

Listen

SECRET. *A heavenly suggestion is to learn to listen to what your body needs and when it needs it.* Honor your physical being. If it is hungry, feed it. If it's thirsty, drink. If you're tired, rest it. Listen. It really is that simple. I know this sounds ridiculous but how many times do we ignore and refuse to acknowledge hunger pains. What happens? You may get a headache, may pop a pill, or lash out at someone, and finally reach for that something that has many calories and no food value.

Trust

SECRET. *Trust your body to tell you what's good for you and what's not.* For example, does your body feel revived after eating sweets or do you get a headache? Do you crave more and more food after you eat carbohydrates, sugar, wheat, or white flour? Your body is overreacting to a particular substances contained in a kind of food. Pay attention to what moods and energy levels accompany what foods. Do you wake up in the morning feeling sluggish? Think what you put into your body the night before. If you ate heavy foods, you may not feel as energetic as you would if you had made other food choices. Don't listen to me, listen to your body. When you want to eat, stop for a moment and see what your body is telling you. What does it really want? It wants satisfaction. You will start taking care of yourself by listening, trusting and becoming aware of your body and what it needs and how it feels, good or not so good. You will respond by making conscious choices, healthier choices. To be educated on food allergies go to: www.MayoClinic.com. It offers a wealth of information.

Address your sweet tooth

If you have a sweet tooth, feed it with something sweet, safe, and natural. Stop when your body says enough. And it will. Listen for it. For years, I didn't know about the sugar blues. I just knew that when I ate chocolate, I ate myself into oblivion and back again, always in the vicious cycle of climbing the scale. When I ate sugar, I literally couldn't stop. If you had tried to take chocolate away from me, I could have committed bodily harm.

I had to have it, it was my fix. It was like a slice of bliss on the road to hell without a happy memory. There was never any relief. Do you relate to any of this? If so, you're already on to a new level of awareness.

> *No NutraSweet™*
> *NutraSweet™ is poison.*
> *If you would like more in-*
> *formation, go to Google and*
> *search out the ill effects.*

A healthy sugar substitute is Stevia. Stevia is a natural herbal sweetener. It is one hundred times sweeter than sugar and is available at any health food store. A little dollop of Stevia goes a long way. If you are stressed and you need to lower your blood pressure, instead of picking up the bar of chocolate, or ice cream, or both do something that nurtures your soul. Raise your energy to a happy vibration by doing something that fills that empty void, such as petting your cat or dog. This is an important behavior change. It gets your mind off the urge to eat sugar and your pet will love it.

If you don't have a pet, whirl around in a circle. Take a shower. Take a walk. Jump up and down for joy. Find humor in something. Call a friend. Do something to get your mind off the food. Then, you can make a choice about what to do next.

To get your body in balance and your food consumption in order, I recommend several options within the guidelines of listening, deciding, and choosing. First, be comfortable with your choices and enjoy what you are doing easily and effortlessly. If you find after a while that what you have chosen does not work, you can change it. Learning to be flexible is a good habit to develop. Quite often people who have food issues are very rigid and controlling, and the idea is to be totally at peace with food so you can begin to deal with other things that will set you free. Food is not your problem. Once you get your mind off the food, you can focus on the things driving you to it. Imagine your new self-image. This book is taking you there.

Unlike diet books or other programs, I'm not going to tell you specifically what to eat or what not to eat. I will suggest though.

What is right for one person is not necessarily right for another. I will tell you what worked for me and seems to be sensible. I will show you the better choices I made. You will choose your own path, and you will release the weight, keep it off, be healthy, be fit and feel fantastic.

When to eat

SECRET. *There is no one and only right way to consume food.* Do you have low periods of energy throughout the day? Eating smaller meals every couple of hours may be better for you. Others are best suited for three meals a day at regular intervals, and snacks in between. Everyone is different. Once you begin paying attention to your body you will be in tune with what your body needs and wants. Your choice will be perfect for you. Just as the sun rises and the sun sets there is breakfast, then lunch, then dinner. Food will be there.

Certain foods will burn the fat. Fried foods and the bad stuff, will not burn fat. Fried foods will make you fat, keep you fat, clog your arteries, and make you ill and very unhappy. Sorry, but true. I don't like saying bad stuff but I said it was a program of honesty. Some foods are better for you than others. Choose foods that will burn fat. More on fat burners later.

No skipping meals

SECRET. *Your body is a machine and needs fuel to run, and if not fed properly and on time the machine wouldn't work at its optimum level.* You will get so hungry you will inhale the wrong foods and fail to establish your new way of eating. This is your goal: to discover the way to eat that nourishes you the most. Here is one of those great **SECRETS** *I discovered along the way: if you want to burn the fat off the body and* *keep it off, fresh green veggies and fish are a great combination.* This is one of the most important sentences in this chapter. You don't like vegetables? Eat them anyway, just like mom said. To add flavor, sprinkle some Spike or Vege-Sal on the greens. Those can be purchased when you get the Stevia at the health food store or the health food section at the grocery store. Not only will you feel mentally clearer and physically lighter as you eat more veggies, you'll wake up full of energy.

When I first began practicing new ways and behaviors, I took containers of cut up celery, cucumbers, peppers, radishes, and clumps of parsley to work. Everyone laughed. I got thinner and they stayed the same. Before long, your co-workers will make comments about how terrific you look and will want to know what you're doing. A large tuna salad with lots of veggies is a great way to burn fat. The more fish and veggies, the better. You're essentially giving your body nutrition and energy. It uses that energy to keep you going, and doesn't store fat. It burns it.

Spend a little time and wash the veggies, put them into containers and eat them when you're hungry. I'm not saying you need to eat celery for six months. I'm saying try some veggies. Steam them, make a salad, toss in some chicken or fish, add some olives. Try something new. You will be spending less money on food and you'll be eating healthier.

> Some vegetables will spoil quicker than others when washed. A quick and easy wash for vegetables is a couple of tablespoons of vinegar with eight ounces of water in a spray bottle. Rinse well and you won't taste the vinegar.

Food preparation

Broil, bake, or roast when cooking meat. Organic meat is better than non-organic with its chemicals and additives. If you are a heavy meat eater, begin adding chicken and fish to your menu. Toss some meat on top of salad, or serve it with rice and beans. Try one meal without meat, and eat grilled or steamed veggies over rice. You'll wake up in the morning feeling light as a feather.

Food shopping

When you go food shopping, purchase enough food for at least several days. You want your food to be as fresh as possible while purchasing a variety of different foods.

SECRET. *Eat different foods every day.* You'll have better weight loss with variety. Looking forward to eating different foods every day is excellent for the body and mind. Boredom will not set in.

The new counting system

This new counting system takes you out of darkness and into heaven. At one time in my life, I was a slave to counting calories and carbohydrates. Counting anything feels ridged and isn't freedom. Would you like to stop counting once and for all? Anything that feels like you have to do it forever is self-defeating. You want freedom in all areas so you can stop living in the grip of insanity. We wouldn't be counting calories or carbohydrates. We will be counting blessings.

SECRET. *The more blessings you count, the more you'll have.* You're on your way to a new lifestyle.

REMEMBER

* Eat to lose
* Choose wisely
* Listen to your body
* Trust your body
* No NutraSweet™
* Fat burners
* No skipping meals
* Food preparation
* Food shopping
* Count your blessings

CHAPTER 5

Fat Eyeballs, Serving Sizes and Choices

KNOWING HOW MUCH is enough cultivates self-confidence and eliminates guessing. This is Heaven. Do you know the expression your eyes are bigger than your stomach? I decided I would take that literally so I got a small inexpensive postage scale. I began to weigh my food, and I pulled out my measuring cup. Together these two items became my new set of eyes. At first a sensible portion, weighed or measured, seemed small. I was sure I'd starve. I found out I had fat eyeballs, and until I began to measure what a portion really was, I didn't realize how much I was consuming. Do you think you have fat eyeballs? **SECRET.** *Weighing and measuring is a great tool in getting food in order.* I did it until my body knew what enough was and then put the scale and measuring cup away. This same process will work for you.

Serving portions

Here's what my serving portions were and gave me what my body needed. I found the portions more than adequate, easy to follow and I lost weight. The serving sizes are broken down in more detail on the menu:

Meats: one serving equals 8 oz for men, 6 oz for women, cooked. Remove skin and fat before cooking. If you are a meat eater, eat a variety of seafood, fowl, and other meats during the week. I would recommend eating at least five seafood meals a week, and remember that

beef is the heaviest meat. Ultimately, listen to your body's wisdom.
· *Fruit:* one serving equals one piece or 1/2 cup for berries
· *Cheese:* one serving equals 1 oz
· *Cottage cheese:* one serving equals 2 oz
· *Milk:* one serving equals 8 oz
· *Bread:* one serving equals 1 slice
· *Cereal:* one serving equals 1/2 cup
· *Eggs:* one serving equals 1 egg
· *Nuts/Seeds:* one serving equals 1 oz
· *Sugar vegetables:* one serving equals 4 oz
· *Other vegetables:* one serving equals 1 cup

Eat less, and eat more of the healthy foods. A postage scale takes out the guessing, and after a while you'll begin to trust yourself, and you'll stop obsessing over the portions. You will just know, and when you know, you can put the scale away forever.

Alkaline/acidic foods

Now is a good time to mention the importance of eating more foods that are alkaline rather than acidic. The reason you want to eat more alkaline foods is to balance the PH in your body. Chances are that disease can't live in an alkaline body; your body should be more alkaline to create a healthy environment. And while we do need some acid, we don't need an acidic body.

I am not a nutritionist or a doctor. To understand and educate yourself regarding balancing the PH in your body, I suggest an excellent book, **Alkalize or Die** *by Dr. Baroody.* This book explains it all: the reasons, the foods which are preferred, and how emotions affect the physical body. An excellent resource.

What follows is a list of the many healthy foods that will change the way you look and feel.

I. MEAT & SEAFOOD

A. Seafood
bass
butterfish
catfish
cod
tuna
flounder
halibut
haddock
lobster
mahi-mahi
orange roughy
perch
pike
salmon
scallops
shrimp
swordfish
snapper
trout
tilapia
whitefish

B. Fowl
chicken
turkey
duck
cornish hens

C. Game meat/ other
elk
venison

mutton
goat
ostrich
bison

D. Beef
steak
hamburger
hot dogs (all beef)
roast beef
ribs

E. Pork
chops
ribs,etc.

II. FRUITS

A. Fruits
apples
apricots
avocado
bananas
berries
cherries
cranberry
dates
figs
grapes
grapefruit
kiwi
lemon
lime
mangos
melons
nectarines
oranges
pomegranates
persimmons
peach
papayas
plums
pineapple
pears
prunes
raspberries
strawberries

B. Sugar Vegetables
butternut squash
beets
brussels sprouts
carrots
corn
green beans
lima beans
leeks
onions
parsnips
peas
tomatoes

III. VEGETABLES

alfalfa sprouts	endive	parsley
asparagus	escarole	peppers
bamboo shoots	fennel	pimentos
bean sprouts	garlic	radishes
bok choy	ginger	spinach
broccoli	jicama	squash
cabbage	kale	swiss chard
cilantro	kohlrabi	turnips
celery	lettuce	watercress
cucumbers	mushrooms	water chestnuts
eggplant	okra	zucchini

IV. GRAINS/CEREAL

barley	rice bread	whole grain
couscous	rice cakes	cereal – no added
essene bread	rye bread	sugar
cornbread	spelt bread	
oats	wheat bread	

V. BEANS/LEGUMES/SOY

aduke	lentils	soy
black beans	pinto	soy milk
black eyed peas	white beans	tofu
fava	couscous	

VI. NUTS/SEEDS

almonds	walnuts	almond butter
cashews	pine nuts	peanut butter
hazelnuts	pumpkin seeds	cashew butter
peanuts	sesame seeds	etc.
pecans	sunflower seeds	

Choosing the best quality of foods

Unfortunately, food quality is not as high as it once was. Not so long ago, the soil was richer and imparted more nutrients into food, and the world had less chemicals. Ideally, it is best to purchase organic food, but it is pricey. If you're not able to buy organic, buy only fresh fruits and vegetables and use the vinegar and water solution for cleaning. Canned or frozen foods simply don't provide the amount of nutrients your body needs. It's easier to prepare them but we are making better choices now. When food is cooked, processed, or canned, the nutritional value goes way down. It may take a little time to get used to your new ways but you will benefit and your body will crave the live foods.

It's a good idea to take food supplements, but the truth is you don't have to purchase anything. You can get your food in order without buying other products. Keep it simple for now because you have lots of new things to think about. Perhaps if you wanted try a good multi-vitamin or Juice Plus. Juice Plus is freeze-dried fruits and vegetables in a capsule and I've been consuming it for years. I love that product. A multi-vitamin and Juice Plus both would be a great beginning.

Juice Plus is offered by NSA. Imagine over seventeen fruits and vegetables freeze-dried in small capsules. This doesn't take the place of eating fruits and vegetables but it's in addition to them. Hair and nails grow faster, your energy level stays up, and it helps balance blood sugar. If you'd like to try Juice Plus, order it from my website: www.DietsDontWorkYouDo.com

Healthy food suggestions

Choose variety. Alternate eating meat, chicken, and fish along with different vegetables. Reduce your red meat meals to three per week then alternate the fish and chicken. If you're not a red meat eater, alternate fish and chicken. If you are a vegetarian, choose legumes, tofu, nuts and seeds for your protein sources along with eggs and dairy if you eat them.

When I got serious about making life changes, I ate three meals a day and snacks in between. I then experimented with six smaller meals to see how that felt. Now I eat three meals with lots of snacks when I want. In time, you'll find out what is right just for you. Again, your body will let you know.

Remember why you are weighing and measuring, to get your portions reasonable. It is temporary, until you trust yourself and know when "enough is enough." When using your scale, take into account the weight of the container that you are using, and remember that meat shrinks during cooking.

Again, a sample menu has been provided at the end of the Physical section. It will send you off to an excellent start. You'll eventually be comfortable eating without any restrictions or limitations. **SECRET.** *Freedom means learning to listen to your body.*

Healthy choices

Eat whole grain breads and the darker the better. White bread has virtually no nutritional value. It is merely empty calories and carbohydrates. If you are eating out at lunch, you may want a roll. Have it. Enjoy it. When you write your food plan, you have made the decision so there is no guessing and no guilt. The important thing is that you've written it down. We have to nip guilt with the diet word. There is freedom and pure enjoyment in your future days.

Eat the unlimited vegetables at any mealtime and snack. Great not to count calories, isn't it? And remember, the combination of any of these veggies and fish will burn the fat.

When eating sugar vegetables, eat them only at dinner in four ounce portions. They will help to carry you through the evening, keeping your energy stable.

A serving of avocado is one small at each meal. Avocados are full of the good kind of fat, and great nutrients. They have even been shown to keep cholesterol down.

Unlimited drinks: water, tea, coffee, club soda with a twist of lemon or lime. If you feel anxious or feel as if you're racing through life, you may consider giving up the caffeine and switching to decaffeinated beverages. Coffee was one of the first things I eliminated and I could feel the difference immediately. I don't miss it, though I never gave up tea.

Whatever you choose, enjoy. Go easy on yourself when making changes.

Unlimited spices and condiments: salt, pepper, herbs, all spices, vinegar, white preferred or better than vinegar, lemon. You can always go heavy on the garlic, easy on the salt.

A great snack is a shake made of either cow or soy/rice/almond milk and a piece of fruit blended with some ice cubes. The ice cubes make it thick, and it's filling. Often I add pecans, protein powder, a couple pieces of fruit, or yogurt, and I'm good for hours. You'll learn to make them, and enjoy them as much as you think you enjoy that chocolate shake. Be patient.

Best to limit eggs to four a week. One for breakfast or two for lunch. Try an egg salad sandwich with fresh parsley, mustard, chopped celery, and garlic powder.

I know you're asking, "What about this food and what about that food." I only include foods that are excellent choices and your body will let you know. A do not eat list is negative. Let's just say the above is your new list for the moment. You'll be eating more than you're eating now, much more nutritiously, losing pounds and getting your food under control. Are you feeling optimistic? You'll be totally satisfied in many ways. No more diets. Ever.

I know there are many prepared foods on the market to help you lose weight. Here is my opinion: they are expensive and you don't need them. It is a big business, and while there is nothing wrong with making money in business, there are other options.

Also, I question how healthy they are. Read the ingredients, and if you can't pronounce them don't buy it. Those ready-made meals are often loaded with additives and chemicals which aren't good for you, and they also set you up to want to eat more. Have you tried eating those pre-packaged meals and lost weight, only to gain it back? All of us have tried all kinds of methods; all of us have lost weight and many of us have gained it back.

REMEMBER

*   Weigh and measure
*   Serving portions
*   Alkaline/acidic foods
*   Food selection
*   Choose the best
*   Juice Plus
*   Healthy food suggestions
*   Healthy choices

CHAPTER 6

Power Tools
to Create the New You

♥

TOOL 1. Create a menu plan with variety

An excellent way to develop a better relationship to food is to create a menu plan. You can plan for a day, a week, or a month, whatever works for you, your family, and your lifestyle.

Choose different foods daily. **SECRET.** *Our bodies love change.* When I ate a variety of different foods each day, I lost weight. Eating a variety of food helps you from getting bored; boredom could set you up for a turn down a path you don't want to travel. Actually, it's not a wrong path, just a different one temporarily. And while it's important to chose a different menu daily, some foods are so good and so healthy you can probably eat them until the cows come home and never tire of them. You can eat them knowing they will give you energy and your body will love you for it. What foods? Veggies, of course. Please begin eating veggies today. Oops, I just told you what to do. Excuse me. A gentle remember: the more you eat of the "fat burners", the more you lose.

TOOL 2. Getting off track...getting back on

We all get off track. **SECRET.** *Expect that you will get lost from time to time; that is part of the process.* When this happens, get back on the road that feels good. The first step is recognizing that the path you're on isn't where you want to be. The next step is realizing that getting to the one you want is relatively easy. A choice, taking action, a step in the right direction and there you are on the new path. With the information you're learning, you have the resources to get back on the right track quickly. You'll ask for help, get it, and move on. **SE-CRET.** *And every time you get off track, you will learn something about yourself, something beneficial.*

I had a devastating experience after a long time away from binge-ing. It was during one of those lows at the end of a relationship, always a prime time for emotional eating. I was in such emotional pain over the loss of my love that nothing else penetrated. I had thirteen months of eating sensibly, making healthy choices, walking a path that was healthy and kept me feeling good. I was convinced I was cured of insanity and that food would never be a problem again. Wrong.

One morning, I found myself sitting under a tree on the grounds of St. Anne's Catholic Church, on the corner of Westheimer and Sheppard in Houston, Texas. It was as if some entity took over my body and I was once again in the act of obsessive-compulsive behavior and could not stop. Pushing grief, sadness and loss down with food, I ate myself into oblivion with watermelon and almonds until my stomach hurt. While anything would have been a nasty slip, and would have signified a binge, watermelon and almonds aren't meant to be eaten together. The bloat I experienced, that didn't want to come out, suffice is to say that I thought I would die. After the binge, I was truly devastated. Because I hadn't binged in over a year, I thought I was fixed, that all of my problems in life were solved. That was because I thought food was my problem.

For the next year and a half, I took many turns but that first one was the worst because it came as a shock, totally unexpected when I thought I had everything under control. In fact, I didn't have anything under control. It wasn't until I learned the connection between food and emotions, and learned to look beneath the behavior, that things started to make sense and I began to heal.

I know you'll hop back on the trail when you stray from it, and the day will come when food will never be a problem again for you. If you stay with these suggestions and absorb the **SECRETS**, *you'll get results*. My promise once again. You will eat to enjoy and to be healthy, look and feel fabulous, and weigh what you want. Isn't that a fantastic thought? Not only is it a fantastic thought, you are now in the process of creating that reality for yourself.

When I write those words, it makes me feel deeply and profoundly grateful. I still take wrong turns in my life and I travel places that don't put a smile on my face, but it has nothing to do with food. When I stop long enough to look in the mirror, at the problem and the situation, I bounce back pretty quickly. So will you. Time to get down to some nitty gritty action.

TOOL 3. Take a picture of yourself

"Do I have to?" you ask. Highly suggested. You need a good honest comparison for the future. Have someone take a full length picture of you. You may not want to do it but it's important. Put the picture in view and look at it often. You won't be able to make excuses or pretend anymore. Once you make that commitment, you are on your way. Be gentle and kind with yourself. No name calling, no recriminations. You are your own best friend in this, and you wouldn't call your best friend names.

You may find yourself blaming your bones. "I'm fluffy because I have large bones." You might rationalize that since your entire family is fluffy, you're fluffy also. There's the glandular problem. Maybe I'm fluffy because I had babies. No more excuses. If you hang on to them, you'll hang on to the weight and you'll have more of the same: no changes, more confusion and despair. Getting honest gets you healthier faster. If you still can't snap that photo, that's OK. Take the photo when you can. And no matter what, do not beat yourself up.

TOOL 4. Journaling

An excellent way to approach the new you is to have a journal for your daily activities, for recording food planning and menus, for your thoughts, resistance, successes, and emotions around food and eating. You can easily refer to your journal to review your previous menus. You can use a plain notebook, you can pick one up at your favorite store, or you can create one of your own. Make it fun, make it easy, and choose something that appeals to you. Honor your process.

Suggestions on how to set up your journal:
On the left page of your notebook write everything pertaining to food.
On the right page, write everything pertaining to your feelings and emotions.
Perhaps from the back forward, set aside space for the things you are grateful for daily. At least five things daily but as many as you want.

Writing your food down will not be forever just as weighing and measuring won't be. I have the original book I started many years ago, kept as a reminder of what I have accomplished. To see where I was then compared to where I am now is a miracle. I was so precise in those days. It helped me get well. Being well, being free, starts with creating new behaviors. Just how long can you expect to write in your food journal? As long as it takes you to get results. It will be different for everyone. It took me a good year. I would imagine for some that would seem a long time, for others a short time. The time isn't important, the results are. I was willing to do what it took. Are you willing to do what it takes? I know you are. View my old journal.

at www.DietsDontWorkYouDo.com/journal.html

A familiar saying: it's the journey not the destination. Life is forever. Please relax.

Choose morning or evening to write in your food journal, depending on your schedule and what feels right for you. Mornings might be best for a number of reasons: you won't have to think about it for the rest of the day; you'll set yourself up to get through the day without constant thoughts of food; and if you wait until evening, other commitments may get in your way. You want to be focused and clear as you create your new ways. Do this with a sense of take charge. Make it fun.

You could select your food choices for the entire day and place them in columns. For example, write down all the food you'll eat for breakfast, your snack, lunch, snack, dinner, and snack. Be specific and write the proper weight and measurement amounts. If it's meat, write 6 ounces cooked not just meat. Carrots, write 4 ounces raw not just carrots. Write down every single thing you're going to put into your mouth. The sample menu at the end of this chapter is based on three meals a day with snacks in between.

There is another important reason for writing in your journal besides freeing yourself from food thoughts for the day. **SECRET.** *Commitment.* You are going to be accountable to yourself. You gave your word to yourself, now you are expected to keep it. Quite often people who have food issues have tendencies to be irresponsible. Do you think you are irresponsible? I admit, I was. Honesty is painful and healing. Contradictions.

TOOL 5. The Magic Key

You may have heard of similar food tracking before, but I've added a new piece, the magic key. This is my **SECRET.** *I believe it was* *the most important key in unlocking my dilemma around food.* When I started doing this, my heart began to open and I began to experience magic in my life. I began to believe there truly was an answer to my problem which for so long seemed to have no solution. I began to see the light.

Just what did I do? The magic I wrote on the top right corner of every page of my food journal was TGA, which meant, Thank you God for my abstinence. For me, this recognized the Higher Power and acknowledged the gift of freedom from compulsion. Your acronym might be different. It could be TY, for Thank you, or IG, I'm grateful, or simply IFGT, I feel great today. Create your own acronym and insert it in your journal. For a very long time, I was unable to say the word God. I say it often now.

TOOL 6. Importance of having a buddy

A buddy, a person who has the same intensity and determination to change as you do to. **SECRET.** *This person can help you stay on track and listen with an open heart.* You in turn will be there for him or her. I know you have friends who want to lose weight. More people than not are weight conscious, or at least talking about it. When people open up to themselves and to others, it is amazing what happens. It's almost like magic when you realize you're not alone in your quest. Approximately thirty-three million people in the U.S. are miserable over their food issues. Let's help one another. **SECRET.** *Helping is healing.*

TOOL 7. Visit my blog

It was designed to create a healing, safe and supportive environment. I will regularly post information, answers to your questions, inspirational material, and I want to hear your stories and concerns. Additionally, you'll hear from others who are wrestling with similar problems over food. You'll hear what they have to say about becoming stronger, slimmer, and healthier. You'll be moved by their stories, experiences, and successes at www.DietsDontWorkYouDo.com.

You will be amazed at the value of having a buddy and getting on the blog. What a tremendous support they both are.

REMEMBER

*   Get off track, get back on
*   Take a picture
*   Journaling
*   The magic key
*   Buddy system
*   Visiting my blog

CHAPTER 7

Family,
Determining and Maintaining
Weight Loss, Exercise

❤

THIS COULD BE a touchy topic, your friends and family. Do you feel pressured around your family and friends? I used to try to explain why I didn't eat certain foods and people would look at me as if I had a screw lose. Some people may not want you to lose weight because it will change their relationship with you. Our loved ones often think they are loving us by offering unhealthy food, or food in large amounts. When it's offered you may say, "I couldn't eat another bite." If the pressure continues, and it probably will, you may have to say "no thank you" and hold to that without explanation and not back down. Be prepared that your friends and family might take it personally, and you might want to think about how to talk to them, how much you appreciate and love them. But you need to take care of yourself by not eating whatever they're offering. I come from an Italian background and I don't know any Italian who doesn't enjoy food. Actually, I don't know many people who don't enjoy food. Do you?

My mother didn't accept the fact I had severe problems with food. "Mangia, mangia, mangia" was her motto. She couldn't understand why I choose not to eat certain things. I had to say no a lot. I felt foolish for a while but I got over it and it got to be funny. I knew the script by heart as we played the same roles over and over. Food was the prime focus in our daily lives as I grew up, and it's not a surprise to me that food became a problem. How was it in your family?

Your loved ones simply may not understand this process. That's alright. By now you have developed an acute awareness of when your body feels good, and when it doesn't. **SECRET.** *You know what's right for you.* That doesn't mean it has to be right for anyone else and you don't have to explain yourself, make excuses, or tell fibs.

Take care of yourself first and then introduce new things into your home gradually. If you have to prepare two different meals, that's perfect, you can do that. Soon they'll see results and will be interrogating you on certain foods you're choosing. You are becoming the new role model.

How to determine your weight loss

How much weight will you lose? When you follow your new food plan, expect to lose approximately four pounds the first week then an average of two pounds a week depending on how much you need or want to lose. It will happen.

Next question on your mind: how much should I weigh? That is a great question. To see Met Life insurance guidelines please visit, www.DietsDontWorkYouDo.com/weightcharts.html. The information will guide you regarding your height and frame. Remember these numbers are only a starting point; insurance guidelines are notoriously too low. The most important guide is your own body; if Met Life says 130 is your perfect weight but you feel best at 140, choose 140.

If you need to lose more than ten pounds, think of losing five pounds and then gauge yourself from there. That will keep you going. Set your goal. Write it down in your journal where you can view it many times during the day. When you reach a plateau and you will, you'll you feel as if your weight won't budge another pound, wait it out. Trust that when you keep eating healthy, you'll reach a point where your weight will start to drop again. It could be one week, it could be two, three or longer. Expect this.

SECRET. *Your body chemistry is adjusting to the weight loss and balancing the changes in your body.* It's taking a time out. Chances are, even though you know to expect the plateau, you'll still be frustrated. This is usually a critical time for people and often they give up. Remember that you have a choice to be frustrated or to accept. Choose acceptance. Other things are happening. Your body is redistributing your weight and your measurements are changing. Stay with your new changes and the weight will begin to come off again.

Are you wondering how often to weigh yourself? I recommend that you weigh yourself once a week, and record your progress. If you are stable on a plateau, record that in your journal. You will from time to time review your progress and it will help you gauge how far you've come. Congratulate yourself.

When I was in the grips, I didn't have just one scale, I had two. If I didn't like what one was showing, I went to the other for reassurance. I suspect you'll find this hard to believe; then again perhaps you won't, depending how obsessive and insane you are, if you are obsessive or insane. When I was in the depths of insanity, I was obsessed with the scale, just as I was with putting those little beads from the diet pills into the capsules. I jumped on and off the scale numerous times during the day, ten times in an hour. Can you see that in your minds eye? Fast forward the picture and watch that person go from room to room, jumping on and off the scale. I wonder if anyone has ever coined the term, scale addiction?

I have not owned a scale for over twenty five years and you will eventually reach a point where you may give yours up, too. Not owning a scale is freedom!

You are beginning to blossom and becoming more beautiful each day. Let's pretend you've arrived. It feels wonderful doesn't it? It is a dream come true, and you did it. You have shed the pounds and you are happier, healthier, and feeling great. You have finally made peace with food. You have learned to eat the proper foods and proper amounts in a well balanced way.

SECRET. *Imagine having a switch hidden somewhere in your body that turns off when you've had enough food.* We all have one and you'll feel it go off. "Enough is enough". That's when deep satisfaction sets in. You wouldn't want to eat another bite. Promise.

How to maintain your ideal weight

How many times have you lost weight and felt so pleased? Then before you knew it, the weight began to creep on again and more. You've taken a different path this time so it will be different. Your weight loss is permanent. You are now going into a new phase, called maintenance. Maintenance is for life. It is time to take a picture of the new you, or take that first picture if you skipped that part. The day has come that the image you have visualized in your mind over the months is now matching the new you. It is easier to take this picture now, isn't it? Carry it around and take it out. Aren't you pleased, thrilled, happy? Look often at your progress. Share it with others to inspire them.

This is your opportunity to remain at your desired weight, within your normal fluctuations, around five pounds, give or take a few throughout the rest of your life. You need guidance and patience. Here is where it may get a little shaky. But there's no turning back now, only more rewards in the future. After understanding the other sections and putting what you've learned into practice, you are beginning to live life in a new and different way, filled with confidence and a knowing that you have overcome the insanity of food issues.

Introducing foods into your body

Once you've reached the goal you've chosen, you're ready to introduce some of the foods which have not been on your list for awhile. If you slowly and cautiously introduce them back in your new way of eating, you may continue to lose. And, you can get on the blog for help, support, and encouragement. I wouldn't suggest doing this alone. As you needed and wanted help in the beginning I was there, I'm here now as well. I'm committed to your success. Since everyone's body chemistry is different, some people will tolerate foods and the amounts consumed differently. What may work for one person may not work for another. There are no rules. As you reintroduce the foods you have put aside, listen to your body's reaction and pay attention to how you feel. You want your body to absorb the food and turn it into energy without a weight gain. If there is a weight gain, be patient as you're fine-tuning your machine. You're experimenting.

Quite possibly you are being triggered by a particular food; put that food aside and try it some other time. Trigger foods are foods that make you want to overeat or binge. Be aware of your body's reaction to sugar, wheat and flour; you may discover specific trigger foods. Keep experimenting with other foods, again being alert to the reaction. Clear thinking and feeling energized is a wonderful way to travel throughout life. It's important to remember to be gentle with yourself; this is going to take some time. **SECRET.** *Learning to maintain isn't an overnight process, just as learning to eat well and resolving food issues wasn't.* As you slowly introduce new foods, you'll find your body will thrive on them.

Be aware of the difference between wanting because you want it now, and wanting because you used to want it. As strange as it sounds, you may find that you do not want the foods you put aside. Since I learned to eat healthy foods, I no longer want the icky foods. My body doesn't crave them anymore. You too may reach a point where your body doesn't want certain foods.

Sometimes I do choose to eat sweets. There is a restaurant in Houston that has the very best cheesecake in the world. I eat it when I go there and it's a treat, even though for the most part I don't eat sugar. Your special cheesecake will be different. You may have something like this, that one thing that you eat every time you eat out. If you are still hiding that stash of candy bars or chips, go to the stash and eat one. Don't feel guilty, just know that occasionally this is fine. **SECRET.** *Your body will tell you when you've had enough.* Listen to your body. I couldn't eat the cheesecake all the time, nor would I want to, but every now and then, it is definitely worth it. I love it and enjoy it without any twinges of guilt and it does not trigger a binge. You're fine tuning your body also.

You may find that a certain food seduces you beyond words. I suggest that's one food to eat only outside your home. Or, you may choose to let go of it completely. It is always your choice. For example, I decided not to eat chocolate many years ago. That was my cocaine. It isn't in my reality any more. This is how that came about.

Nine years after my diet pill epiphany, I lost the weight I wanted to lose and was cooking my Aunt Princine's birthday dinner. Of course, we sampled from Friday until Sunday. What I mean by sampling is we ate and ate and ate. Before the party, I was so full I had to undo my pants. I ate all over again once the party began. Can you relate? Finally, it was Birthday cake time and I dove into the huge chocolate cake covered with gooey white frosting like there was no tomorrow. Food was coming out of my ears. Even though my poor body was about to burst, I couldn't stop eating the cake. I heard a voice that got louder and louder: "this chocolate is making me crazy, I can never eat it again." It wasn't water that I was retaining, it was chocolate! Over the years, I've not wanted it or been tempted. Is chocolate still being made? I don't know.

Giving up chocolate did indeed help, but it didn't cure my eating issues. I was still compulsive. **SECRET.** *There may come a time when you will make the decision, not necessarily with chocolate but with something else, to let it go.* It may even be a person or a job. As you read this, you may know now what I am talking about. Deep down you know, you are all-knowing. All things in time.

A midnight snack suggestion

Here is suggestion you may want to try when experimenting with *maintenance*. I found this to be very helpful. When I have a light snack before I go to bed, I sleep better. I'm not talking about a full course meal. I often have fruit and cheese or some nuts. **SECRET.** *It keeps the blood sugar level stable during the night.* A friend who is a nurse passed this on to me and now it's yours. It helps me and I think it will help you too.

Rewarding yourself

Now it's time to shop. One can never, never, never have enough pairs of shoes! There are some lovely obsessions. Yes, reward yourself with those wonderful clothes you thought you would never wear. Let this be an incentive to keep the weight off, and a reminder for you to keep on your new way of eating and living. Looking great and feeling great are what you have strived for. Looking at the picture of the new you is never tiring, is it? Huge congratulations, again and again. Enjoy.

If the pill episode was my first awakening, the cake episode was the second. Four years later, I began writing TGA, Thank you God for my abstinence in my journal. Yours will probably be different. From then to now has been the most profound, deeply moving time in my life, and I'm not done yet. **SECRET.** *Every day is a new beginning for all of us.*

Exercise

Exercise is vital for our body's health, but you don't have to exercise like a fool or spend tremendous amounts of money at expensive fitness clubs. Being mindful of what goes into our bodies and how we treat them is key to maintaining excellent, radiant health. My happy pills today are Hatha Yoga and Dance. Find something you really enjoy and do that. Put some music on and move. Let it take you to new places of self-expression. It's your time. Exercising our minds is equally important. As the book unfolds, you'll discover new techniques to stimulate brain power.

Regading this entire process, if you are ready that's perfect, and if you aren't sure, that is perfect also. Please keep reading. **SECRET.** *We all have our time for awakening.* Something deep inside is calling you toward a new way of living and being. Remember to be gentle and easy with yourself. Healing will come to you at the most perfect time. **Lighten Up** addresses all of you. You are stepping into your Greatness. You're changing as your read these words. We grow to the degree we want to grow. But wanting to grow is not just something that can waft casually through our minds once a week, or once a day when we come to meditation. It must become an ongoing living reality. It's the depth from which we want to grow that makes it begin to unfold.

"We grow to the degree that we mobilize resources that we may not even know we have at the moment. But because we deeply want to grow, because we have this deep passion for knowing God, because we have this love of life and love for God, then that love itself becomes a living event within us. It demonstrates every kind of potential to overcome obstacles, to overcome barriers, to move mountains. It certainly allows us to discover within ourselves vast, unrecognized treasures. In cultivating it, countless extraordinary capabilities organize themselves within us, and manifest for the purposes of our liberation and fulfillment."
Swami Chetanananda, *The Breath of Life.*

Meal/Day	Monday	Tuesday	Wednesday	Thursday	Friday	Saturday	Sunday
Breakfast	1 egg 1 slice bread 1 grapefruit	2 oz cottage cheese 1 slice bread Cantaloupe	1c. cereal 8 oz. milk 1 slice bread 1/2 banana	2 oz. cottage cheese 1 slice bread 1 grapefruit	1 slice cheese 1 slice bread 2 plums	1 egg 1 slice bread 1 orange	1c. cereal 8 oz. milk 1 nectarine 1 slice bread
Snack	1 cup milk 1 apple	1 oz almond Butter 1 banana	4 oz berries 1 oz almonds	1 oz sun-flower seeds 8 oz tomato juice	1 apple 8 oz yogurt	8 oz kefir 1 oz pump-kin seeds	1 tbs peanut butter w/ celery
Lunch	4 oz cottage cheese 1 slice bread Unlimited veggies	1/2c. rice 1c. beans 1 slice bread Unlimited veggies	4 oz flounder 1 slice bread Unlimited veggies	2 eggs 1 slice bread Unlimited veggies	4 oz tuna 1 slice bread Unlimited veggies	6 oz chicken 1 slice bread Unlimited veggies	4 oz cottage cheese 1 slice bread Unlimited veggies
Snack	1 tbs cashew butter w/celery	1 oz pump-kin seeds 1 pear	8 oz grapes 1 oz cashews	1/2 canta-loupe 1 slice cheese	2 oz cottage cheese 8 oz kefir	1 peach 1 oz cashews	4 oz pine-apple 1 oz almonds
Dinner	6 oz salmon 4 oz peas Unlimited veggies	6 oz chicken 4 oz carrots Unlimited veggies	6 oz roast beef 4 oz green beans Unlimited veggies	8 oz tofu 1 cup rice Unlimited veggies	6 oz turkey 4 oz potato Unlimited veggies	6 oz perch 4 oz Brussels sprouts Unlimited veggies	1/2 cup rice 1 cup beans Unlimited veggies
Snack	8 oz kefir 1 orange	8 oz milk 1 slice cheese	1/2 banana 8 oz yogurt	1 cup milk Nectarine	4 oz berries 1 oz sun-flower seeds	Milkshake w/3 dates	4 oz straw-berries 8 oz yogurt

Food is not your problem

Food is your substitute for all the things in life you want and don't have

Commit never to diet again

Give up artificial sweeteners and diet pills

When you get off track get back on the same day

Diets Don't Work YOU Do

You'll find your treasure; you are on your way

REMEMBER

* Being influenced
* Determine weight loss
* Maintenance
* Introduce foods slowly
* Snack before bedtime
* Rewarding yourself
* Exercise just for you

PART III

THE MENTAL

Changes from the inside out

♥

CHAPTER 8

Get Honest With Yourself

IF YOU'RE ANYTHING like the way I was, what I thought about myself and how I dealt with life was another underlining cause of my problem with food. Could it be that food is your drug of choice you use to numb your pain? That question never entered my mind when I ran over those hot coals in Hell.

In the Physical Part, I asked general questions regarding food and now I'm going to take you in another direction. Please take some time to think about the following questions. **SECRET.** *You may discover some things about yourself that may surprise you and may begin to open you up in new exciting ways.*

Are you honest with your feelings? Does fear run you, fear of success and fear of failure? Have you been in and out of relationships unable to sustain them in healthy ways? Do you have money issues? Are you are afraid of life? Do you feel like a failure? Do you dislike or even stronger, hate how you look, how you act? Do you criticize yourself unmercifully? Do you feel unworthy, not good enough, unwanted, underserving? Do you put everyone else before you? Are you a people pleaser? Do you have a voice, asking for what you need, asking for what you want? Do you feel loved? Are you obsessive? Do your thoughts and feelings drive you to insanity? Do they drive you to food?

You know what to do with your physical self: the actual eating part, the food journal, the veggies, being active, all the rest. As you begin to shed the layers of your being that don't serve you in positive ways, both your food issues and the weight will fall away as well.

Instead of food as a way to deal with life, you will have tools to help you live to your fullest potential. Your self image will be one of confidence and strength. How you think, react and deal with life will complement your new physical being. **SECRET.** *How you live on the inside will reflect on how you live your life on the outside.* I know by now you are beginning to experience some interesting insights along with gaining new knowledge. This new way of thinking and being will continue as you delve deeper into **Lighten Up. SECRET.** *YOU are the answer to your success.*

I walked around in a thin body for quite a while before I learned much of what I'm going to share with you. **SECRET.** *Being thin does not mean being well.* If I had known this information sooner, my process would have been accelerated. But I didn't. I believe we all arrive in our own time. Now that you have the plan laid out for your food, let's begin to create more miracles in other areas of your life.

Self-Image

SECRET. *Everything you have, everything you want, everything you are getting and everything you are not getting, are all connected to your self image.* How do you think and feel about yourself and about this thing called life? Your self image is connected to whatever you do in your life, what you judge to be good and not so good. For example, if you think you are fat and will never lose weight, that is precisely what will show up. I realize this is a strong statement. However, as soon as you begin to change your thoughts, knowing you can be in a new healthy body and feeling great about it, you'll begin to experience a new life with these precise changes coming to fruition. How you begin to change your thoughts will be addressed in a greater way further along in the book. For now, we are in the process of laying a solid foundation for exciting and life-altering changes. Let's begin by accepting several important facts.

Be here now

SECRET. *We only have NOW.* The past is gone. We may visit it occasionally in order to get some valuable information and enjoy wonderful memories, but we don't want to live there. Everything you have ever done, thought, or experienced has brought you to where you are, so keep what serves you. Tomorrow is uncertain, and while our plans are important, they are simply plans.

Don't play the game of "I will be happy when: I get my bills paid off, when the right person comes into my life, when I get my new job, when I lose weight." **SECRET.** *At any given moment we have the ability to change an act, a thought, a behavior, a direction, an anything.* Don't wait. Be happy now.

How to begin to create change

SECRET. *What you think and what you do make this moment what it is and if you want to change, change what you think and do.* When you have food thoughts, are they because your body is telling you it's time to eat? That it's hungry? If not, what are your needs, wants, and your real hunger? If it's not food, it must be something else. Be here now. Ask yourself, "What am I thinking?" "What am I wanting?" "What am I needing?" "What am I doing?" "What are my actions?" If you want love, chocolate won't really give it to you. If you want company, a bag of cookies isn't going to fix that. And if you want a shower, or to feel another person's touch, a bag of chips and dip won't work.

Accept yourself where you are and how you look, right here, right now. You got yourself here for a zillion reasons, and here you are. No more beating yourself up for what you should have done, could have done, what you did do and how it didn't turn out.

Be gentle with yourself. Treat yourself as you would your best friend. Accept that change is possible. Ask yourself, "What do I need to do to take care of myself, become self-reliant and become super powerful?" Yes, super powerful, living your passion. "What do I really want, and how do I want to live my life?" Many people go through their lives and never ask. Now is your chance to begin to live your new life from a higher level of consciousness, and to feel the Power in that kind of thinking. **SECRET.** *It's up to you, not someone outside yourself.* Are you scared and excited at the same time? Accept and embrace it. Create a new life and hold on for a great ride.

Life happens

But what happens when the dododododo hits the fan? Yes, life happens. People come into our lives, and people leave our lives. We get ill, and we get better. We are in control, and we are out of control. We get married, and we get divorced. We marry again. Divorce again. Eek! We gain weight, and we lose weight. Pets leave us, we get another pet. We lose people we love, and we find new people to love. We lose weight, we gain weight. We move, we move again. We lose our jobs and we get better jobs. We win, we lose. We have accidents and we heal. We learn. We grow. We get depressed and we get happy. We gain weight. We lose weight. We gain weight, we lose weight. We hurt. We hurt others. We lie, we cheat, we make amends. We are betrayed, and we love. We hate. We are insane and we are sane. We eat. We starve. We succeed and we fail. We accept, we expect, we cry, we laugh. We lose weight. We make messes in life and we clean up the messes. We drink. We get sober. We do drugs and we get clean. We make money, we save money, we lose money. We make more money. Wow, we're busy.

Life is still going to be life but you are now learning new behaviors to deal with life on your new terms. You won't be complicating it with all those changes, those gains and losses regarding weight. Those concerns are fading away and now Life is becoming more interesting and exciting each day. It does get better and better all the time. **SECRET.** *You create your own reality.*

CHAPTER 9

Daily Steps to Facilitate Change

UNTIL NOW, PERHAPS YOU'VE NOT had the skills or tools to know what to do in everyday situations regarding food, people, and places. You may not have been aware of your feelings and were into the food without any awareness of your actions. Now, all that changes.

These are some simple steps to make it easy. They do require practice. Through these, you'll feel acceptance and strength as you move about in your world. As you learn them, put them in your 'mind pocket', a place of power and safety that you can access at any moment.

STEP 1 Judgment

Stop judging and practice acceptance. We all do it. We judge things right or wrong, good or bad. Start noticing when you make judgments, and stop immediately. Accept things as they are. What is, simply is. Without simple acceptance, you can easily work yourself into a frenzy and make yourself miserable. The pressure is off when you accept things as they are. You're in the moment. Then from acceptance you can ask: What can I do to change it if it's for my highest good? Those contradictions again.

STEP 2 Commitment

Be committed to yourself and others. Do what you say you are going to do, when you say you are going to do it. In Part one, I mentioned writing down your food, daily. That is a perfect example, and a good place to start. When you begin committing and fulfilling your promises to yourself and others, your self-esteem will soar. You become your commitment. When you commit with full intent, you get things going in the direction of your desire. Take the action you need to fulfill your commitments. Practice.

STEP 3 Habits

Drop some habits and create new ones. Look at what you habitually do and think on a daily basis. You may find yourself performing behavior and thinking thought patterns that aren't putting you in a place of empowerment.

A new habit

Send yourself a positive thought on the hours of 3, 6, 9 and 12 during your waking hours.

For example:

I honor myself.

I honor myself and I honor all life.

Keep it simple. Repeat it several times until it drops into your heart. Do this special one message until you want to change it. Make them up, ones that feed your soul. Only one at a time. No matter what you choose, it raises your vibration immediately.

If you're not successful in attaining what you say you want, change the habit. Begin to live differently. Sometimes habits are so ingrained that we're not aware of what we're doing; some habits are healthy, some are not. Perhaps you have a habit of beating yourself up over eating large amounts of food before you go to bed. Change that habit. Eat smaller amounts, and don't beat yourself up. Or do one or the other to start. You may not be in the habit of drinking water; create a new habit of drinking water. Read the food labels. Put other habits on pieces of paper in a box or bag, and pull one out every day and do it. You will find many habits you have, and many you don't. Make changes that feel good. Four simple steps to incorporate daily: Stop judging, accept what is, commit to yourself and to others, and change your habits.

REMEMBER

* Get honest
* Live from the inside out
* Be here now
* Change is possible
* Create change
* Life happens
* Stop judging
* Keep commitments
* Drop some habits
* Create new habits
* Send positive thoughts

CHAPTER 10

Tools for Self-Empowerment

❤

TOOL 1. Halt

Recommended by the 12-step programs

HALT STANDS FOR: Hungry, Angry, Lonely and Tired. When-
ever you find yourself feeling something you're not sure of, or when
you find yourself eating without actively choosing to, halt, and ask
yourself what's really going on now, in the present moment. Let's say
you feel out of sorts, out of balance. You need something.

Hungry

Begin with "*h*", the first letter of halt. Ask, Am I hungry? If the answer is yes, then it may be time to review the information about food,
and go over your food plan. You may need to adjust your eating times
from three meals to three meals with snacks in between. Or perhaps,
your body is wanting six small meals a day. Eating more frequently
could solve those feeling of discomfort. You may even need to adjust
and eat a little more. Allow yourself to be flexible. Being flexible is
freedom. If you begin to get a headache or begin to shake, you've
waited too long. Your body will tell you what it needs. Listen to your
body, a gentle reminder.

Angry

If the answer is no, you aren't hungry, move to "*a* " in halt. Am I angry? My feeling is many of us can answer yes to this question. You are
going to hear a lot about this one because anger is often a big reason
we eat. Stuffing those feelings down with food doesn't allow us to

face our anger, and we don't have to explore what is behind it. When you eat out of anger, the anger shifts to yourself, and you move far from the original cause. But because you didn't address the original cause, you keep eating, stuffing down the new feelings of disappointment, disgust, frustration. You don't even taste the food anymore.

Here's what you do if the answer is the big yes. First, determine who you are angry with; it could be anyone, including yourself, or even a place or a thing. Anger is healthy, an indicator that something isn't right. In our society, we aren't taught to express anger in healthy ways. Often, women hold on to anger, and it comes out in passive, aggressive ways. When I was angry, I often didn't talk, and instead I did inappropriate things to get even with the person I was mad at. This kind of behavior can take many forms as a result of not owning our feelings.

If you're angry, talk to a friend who will truly listen. Maybe that will be enough. Or, talk to the person you're angry with. It's empowering just to say, "I'm angry. What you did made me angry." This may sound like the beginning of a big argument, but it doesn't have to be. Say these things in a normal tone of voice. Expect to feel anxiety, expect to feel afraid, this is normal. Work through that. When you can state your feelings without expecting anything from the other person, you have arrived. Practice with people with whom you feel safe. This may take time but when you begin to cultivate new behavior you will feel strong and confident. You will stop stuffing your feelings with food. Remember, "I'm angry. What you did made me angry." May want to put that in your mind pocket.

There are pitfalls. When you are angry, it's safer for the other person if you don't speak up. The other person has control if you say nothing, or if you say yes all the time. You're not a threat. When you begin to speak up, people will be quite astounded and probably won't like it. But you ask yourself: do you want to be a people pleaser, or do you want to stand in your own power, a place of self-confidence?

Do you want to keep eating when you are angry, or do you want to confront the anger instead? Of course you'll confront the anger. You're courageous.

Lonely

On to the "*l* "in halt. Am I lonely? Yes is the big answer to this one also. If you are lonely, and you eat, you'll still be lonely and you'll also be angry at yourself for eating. Food would taste good, and you would feel better but that's the quick fix and you know better now.

Here are some steps for dealing with loneliness. Call someone. Have a heart to heart talk with a good friend. Open up and just talk. You'll probably find the loneliness dissipate, leaving you feeling validated and heard. Sometimes we need a listening ear. Ask yourself what can you do to help someone else. Reach out to that person. Read something uplifting. Pray. Or simply get acquainted with your loneliness and contemplate the idea that we're never really alone.

Loneliness can be a friend. Welcome those times. They will be different without food. You may feel raw, fearful, scared, vulnerable, or anxious. However, those times will become further apart and short lived. I imagine you may get an aha or two during those lonely times. This is an excellent time to write in your journal. Life changes from moment to moment.

Tired

If the answer is no about being lonely, next is the "*t*" in halt. Am I tired? If the answer is yes and you eat, you'll still be tired, and you'll be angry at yourself for overeating. Same old story, same outcome.

Here are steps to take when you're tired: First, use common sense. If you aren't aware on a conscious level that you are tired, you'll continue to wear yourself down, and try everything other than resting. Try a nap. Or just stop doing what you're doing for a while. Even a little pause will do; take a moment and breath in deeply and slowly, this is very refreshing. Get up and walk away from your desk. Take a break. Get a change of scenery and come back refreshed. Go to bed. In the early days of my recovery, I used to open the refrigerator door and stare inside every time I was tired. I didn't realize I didn't want food. I wanted sleep. Sleep is a good thing. Recharge. Rest. You have choices.

If you're not certain what your feelings are, get out your journal and begin writing. Write anything. Before long your feelings will begin to flow onto the paper. Sometimes things will come up that have been buried for a long time. If you consistently have the same feeling, the same reaction to a certain stimulus, something someone says, or something that happens on a regular basis, chances are it's due to a deep hurt that has been long forgotten. If you can go back to the point where you first felt that feeling, you will find the jewel, the origin. Then magic begins to happens. Once you understand where those emotions and reactions come from, they can be released and be gone forever. Look for an aha or two in your writing and your introspection. They give answers and clues about how you have been behaving. Instead of pushing the feelings down with food, you create an avenue for them to flow into your consciousness for understanding, processing, and release. Magic happens.

TOOL 2. Writing with the opposite hand you write with
This tool is one of the most powerful tools to unleash and release past memories. A long time ago, I learned writing with our non dominant hand, releases memories and images locked in the subconscious mind, bringing them to the surface of the conscious mind. Here is why writing with the non dominant hand is so effective. When writing with your dominant hand, you are in the adult place, feeling confident and sure of yourself. You have control of the writing. When you write with your non dominant hand, it takes you to a place of

vulnerability. It takes us back to being most vulnerable, that of the child. I found the place of the child to be a most sacred place.

One day I decided to try this, to understand why I had felt stupid most of my life, and believed I was a slow learner. I started writing with my left hand and as I wrote, suddenly I had a vivid memory of being in first grade with the teacher holding a long stick with a metal tip on the end. She used it to point to words on a chalkboard: Dick, Mary, Run, Spot. If we didn't know the words, she hit us on the head with the stick. It wasn't even a Catholic school!

I kept writing with my non dominant hand describing her, the situation, how I felt, and I realized that even though I never spoke up in class, I had actually known all of the answers, every time. I wasn't silent because I was stupid or didn't know, it was because I was terrified of her. I was afraid to speak for fear she would hit me on the head. I was afraid to move or open my mouth at all.

After I finished writing, I felt I had been given a gift. Suddenly, I knew I was capable, competent, not slow or stupid at all. Rationally, I had known this all my life, had known that a stupid person could not have actually accomplished all I had accomplished. Yet, the belief that I was slow had run my life for a very long time. Now I looked at myself in profoundly different ways. Something like this can be your experience, too.

TOOL 3. The number 24

This tool helps you get in touch with what you really want. Get a packet of sticky pads. Write the number 24 on lots of individual sheets of papers. Put the individual sheets on your computer, refrigerator, mirrors in your home, your desk at work, and in your car. The next time someone asks you if you can help in planning an event, if you can volunteer, essentially, if anyone asks you anything, you'll have that 24 staring at you. Instead of saying yes immediately, tell the person you'll get back to them in 24 hours. That might be the first time you didn't impulsively blurt out "yes". Spend time thinking about the request. You might decide to do it, or you may realize it isn't something you want to do. You may realize you are tired of being the yes person. Then you can phone your friend back and give your answer: "I have thought about it and I'm going to say no." You have given yourself time, and out of your decision has come power and a new feeling of caring for yourself. You aren't letting anyone talk you into doing something you don't want to do. I say let because no one makes us do anything. **SECRET.** *Remember, we are always at choice.*

TOOL 4. No

A most powerful word with only two letters. Now you are ready for another tool that comes out of a no response. What if your friend says something like, "I can't believe you don't want to do it. You know how we need you, no one can do it like you, you're the greatest, blah...blah...blah." You begin to feel a little weak and may want to give in. If you say "no" again, your friend may very well ask why, and try to make you feel guilty. Your reply is still the same little word, "no". Such a little word with so much power. Remember, when you begin to give an explanation or a reason for your decision, you lose. However, just saying "no" might sound rude; a short firm statement of your reasons is enough, and takes their feelings into account. Example, "No, that doesn't work for me." Or, "No, I'm not doing that at this time. Thank you for asking." Those could be two of your standard replies. Put those in your mind pocket.

TOOL 5. Boundaries

Boundaries are where some of our greatest power lies. Without strong boundaries, we are wimps. Feeling out of control will definitely lead one into the food. I'm constantly reminded to remember my personal boundaries. I sometimes forget. We need to respect the boundaries of others also, and learning our own helps in that as well.

Suggestion, read this information every day for the next month, reinforce it, and you will start to respond in new ways to everyone.

SECRET. *Boundaries are also acts of self-love.* You are saying "enough is enough, no more, stop." Without boundaries, we have no power and as a result often feel like victims. We give our power away to other people who sometimes are demanding and sometimes aren't aware of their actions. When you set boundaries for yourself, you tell people how much respect you have for yourself, that you expect respect and nothing less. From now on, there is no reason or excuse to accept unacceptable behavior from anyone. If you're going to change, care for yourself, grow, and get what you want, boundaries are to be established. Look at your relationships and see where you feel less-than, dominated, or controlled, or maybe all of these feelings. Then set some healthy boundaries. I shall remember my own words.

Sometimes people are preoccupied with their own inner dialogue and aren't able to hear what we're saying. You may have to be very firm: "Stop insulting me, I'm going to leave." "If you hand in your report late again, I'll fire you." Sometimes we're afraid to set boundaries because the fear of losing a loved one or a business deal, or an opportunity is too risky. However, if we don't set boundaries, we lose and food may begin to look very good. That's worse.

TOOL 6. Setting boundaries

Make a list of at least ten boundaries that make you feel empowered and feel great about yourself. They might be as simple as " Not going to answer the phone after 9 pm," or "A 20 minute wait is my limit for anyone." Your boundaries will look different than mine, or anyone else's. Once you have your list, here's how you put them into your life. First, be aware when to apply them. Learn to listen to that sensation in your body that tells you something isn't right with any given situation. You'll feel it in your heart area, or your solar plexus.

Everyone has a built-in guidance system; you may have tuned it out.

You can set your boundaries with others in ways that help the other person learn. This is not permission to lash out at others, but opportunities to stand up for yourself while respecting others, and teach them your boundaries. Some examples of how to speak: "John, stop yelling at me. I do want to hear what you want to tell me. Please lower your voice." Or, "Sarah, when you say you're going to call, I rearrange my schedule to communicate with you. Please call when you say you will."

Remember that your new behavior may not be well received. One thing you have no control over is how people will receive you. The fact that you stand up for yourself is the important issue. You are self-confident and you are communicating that to the other person. **SECRET.** *As with anything, when you begin something new it may be difficult.* Expect to be relatively bad at all this when you first set your limits. When I began to speak up for myself, it came out as me being obnoxious. I wasn't sure what to say because I was used to reacting in other ways. So remember, when you start setting boundaries and speaking up for yourself, it's new behavior, and chances are it may not feel so good. So what? Do it anyway. I promise, the more you set boundaries and speak up for yourself, the more comfortable it will be and the more respect both you and others will have for you. At first try on boundaries with people who are non-threatening. Raise your standards. Be patient and gentle.

By respecting other peoples boundaries, you begin to accept your own, and eventually it's a powerful tool that becomes natural. To honor others and be respectful are equally as important as our own desires. If we want to be spoken to and dealt with kindly, for our highest and best good and for others, then it's our responsibility to speak to others kindly, and deal with them with patience. We don't have to agree yet we can be respectful. We can agree to disagree.

One last point: as adults we have car keys. If the situation gets totally out of control, go ahead and leave for a while. You can always come back when you and others have calmed down.

How long will all this take? And how does it relate to food? Well, how many times have you eaten over not speaking up? How many times have you felt resentment for not saying no, and eaten to numb the feelings? How often have you been angry when someone crossed a boundary you didn't even know you had, and then eaten to quiet the anger?

And no matter how long it takes to get good at this, or to see the results, the first time you set a boundary, the first time you use Halt to effectively identify a feeling, the first time you say no, you will have begun the process of developing your authentic voice. You will know you are making progress when you are feeling empowered in a healthy way. Write those successes in your journal. Setting strong boundaries, feeling safe in your personal space, and learning how to acknowledge and understand your needs lay the groundwork for delving into the deeper you. I congratulate you for your dedicated perseverance in honoring and loving yourself.

Boundaries

Grab those sticky notes and write them down. Stick them on the fridge, on the mirrors, on the doors, on your forehead.

REMEMBER

*   HALT
*   Writing to discover
*   The number 24
*   The power of no
*   Set boundaries

CHAPTER 11

Grow Your Mind

Intentions

A GREAT WAY TO BEGIN each day is by setting intentions, choosing thoughts that are positive, life affirming and filled with gratitude. Set your intentions the moment you open your eyes in the morning to the kind of day you desire to live. You can now begin to choose wisely by preparing your garden of thought as you would plant seeds. This is your sacred garden and begin planting seeds of beauty, and healthy choices to align yourself with the goodness of life each and every day. Here are some uplifting examples for setting intentions.

Say to yourself...
"Today I intend to:
· practice gratitude and look for the good
· have peace around food issues
· listen to my body's needs
· have the courage to ask for what I desire
· attract individuals to help me heal and grow
· spend quality time with my family and friends
· to resolve a conflict with my friend with love and understanding"
A lovely day unfolds as you set your intentions. Be specific for the day and let you imagination soar. We get to have it all. More thoughts about making healthy choices on many levels fill this book. Powerful life-altering information is popping out on every page.

SECRET. *We have desires that are unique to us; they are calling and wish to be fulfilled.* But being in the throes of compulsive behavior, it stops us from knowing what our passion is, let alone pursue it. When we are stuck in a compulsive thought or behavior, it is like banging our heads against a wall that stops the creative flow of anything good to enter our minds. As we realize the wall is just thought, we can shift our thoughts to the sacred garden, the place where we purposefully plant our seeds of life, creativity and goodness. We can make shifts in a moment. You are beginning to swim in a sea of goodness.

Beliefs

What do you believe about yourself? In your eyes, are you intelligent, pretty, cute, beautiful, capable, worthy, handsome, deserving, likable, friendly, humorous, talented, gifted, lovable, safe, secure, comfortable, hopeful, self-confident, happy, strong, supported? Quite often, people who have food issues believe they are stupid, ugly, fearful, unlovable, unworthy, undeserving, unwanted, fat, fat, fat, and on and on and on. This is fertile soil for negative self-talk. If this list hits close to home, you can, for example set an intention for the day to be kind with yourself and praise yourself for the progress you're making.

SECRET. *You're a shining, magnificent star.* We will explore that more in the Spiritual Part but before we get there, let's begin to lay a new foundation by telling yourself some positive, uplifting statements in line with who you truly are. No longer are you going to put yourself down with the negative self-talk, the statements that pull you and your energy down.

Stop the negative self-talk

It is so much of a habit, and takes such subtle forms, that we may not realize we're doing it. Chances are you've been doing it for a very long time and are unaware of it, and all you know is that the chatter in your mind reaches a certain level and you tip over the top. You eat and you have no idea your own voice got you to that point. Start really listening to yourself. If you find you are still talking negatively, as soon as you recognize it, please do the opposite and here's how: immediately state a new, positive statement.

Affirmations

Affirmations are positive statements about you and used as a tool to change your experiences in life. Affirmations will counter the negative statements you've heard and told yourself over the years. At first, they may feel insincere or not about you, or embarrassing to say even if you're alone. What we believe personally has a direct effect on the lives we create. Replace the negative talk with affirmations.

There are two points to saying affirmations

One: State them in the now, not tomorrow, not coming soon, not on the way. Try making your affirmations powerful and in the moment with lots of positive energy. Feel the feeling, get into it, it is now. The subconscious mind is neutral and does exactly what you tell it. Tell it good things. It will obey you either way. Choose consciously. More on the subconscious mind in the Emotional part.

Two: Be honest. When you look in the mirror and have lost weight but still look a little fluffy, it may be difficult to say, "I'm at my perfect weight." It may not ring true. But you can say "I have beautiful eyes, great hair, a lovely smile, and I'm in the process of attaining my perfect weight." It's only a matter of time before the subconscious believes your words. See what feels right for you. You'll know. Create your affirmations.

www.DietsDontWorkYouDo.com/affirmations.html

SECRET. *Affirmations are a great way to lift your mood, which in turn helps to make life more enjoyable.* Make a list and carry it around with you. Get into the habit of saying them often. The more you become aware of when and how you perform negative self-talk, the less you will do it. As with all the tools, place these affirmations in your mind pocket.

Mental Images

Here's how to visualize yourself in the most positive way. Get quiet, perhaps do some deep breathing. Breathing exercises will be addressed in the Spiritual part. For now, close your eyes and picture a mirror in front of you. You're in your own body looking at yourself in the mirror. You're at your ideal weight and wearing the most perfect outfit you can imagine. Turn, smile, dance, look, and take it into your mind. Stay there for at least thirty seconds. Do this often. You are giving your subconscious mind a new image of yourself. One of the most fun mirror exercises I did was seeing myself in a red pants suit, dancing, moving, smiling, laughing. I looked hot and I felt it. Important, the mirror exercise will work best with positive affirmations.

As the Mental part ends, the self-defeating behavior and negative talk ends also. Changes are taking place for your highest good. Your new mantra, the affirmation that starts all others, is: "I think positive, constructive, beautiful and loving thoughts, about myself and about life." You're creating new habits. You have new tools: Setting Intentions, Halt, The number 24, No, Boundaries, Affirmations, Mental Images.

If these new tools are used with discipline and a new level of awareness, many changes will begin to happen within your being and quickly. There is more waiting for you in the pages to come, and in the days and weeks, and years to come. We are always new, always changing, continuing to rediscover who we are. Some say we're on a journey. I say we are the Journey. It is never-ending, so please relax.

You never get it done, life is eternal. You are eternal. You are the best.

I imagine that now you realize or are beginning to realize that the chains that bound you to food didn't have much to do with who you really are. Food has been everything and nothing at the same time; it has been your mask, your way of shielding yourself from the world.

Now the shield is coming down, and the real you is emerging as you are laying a new solid foundation for your new life. **SECRET.** *Changes are from the inside out.*

REMEMBER

*   Set intentions daily
*   What do you belief
*   Stop negative self-talk
*   Affirm positive statements
*   Imagine the best

PART IV

THE EMOTIONAL

There is no precedence in the past

CHAPTER 12

Inner World
of Emotions and Feelings

♥

Emotional triggers

OUR EMOTIONS INCLUDE that vast conglomeration of feelings and reactions that fill our moments and days with joy and acceptance, fear and sadness, and many more emotions. They determine how we live our lives, year after year. And they're not just current feelings, they're the deep-seated emotional scars that many of us carry. They can throw us into the eating cycle without our awareness. Because we don't know how to deal with our emotions and feelings, pain and sorrow, and the unwanted pounds that have resulted, we suffer.

If you're moving through the Physical and Mental parts and you feel confident about your progress with food, you may notice that emotional triggers still come up. **SECRET.** *No matter how secure you are in your newfound outlook, these triggers can sometimes feel almost overwhelming.*

They are supposed to be as they are part of the process. As you move along in the Emotional part, you'll learn many techniques. These techniques will help, my own and others'. These techniques will help you move toward a place of calmness, peace, and serenity. See what feels right for you to explore. **SECRET.** *You may want to explore them all. Remember, you are the journey.* You'll always be challenged by situations, and the purpose of the **SECRETS** *are to give you the power to deal with those situations in positive and healthy ways, without using food.*

REMEMBER

* No power in the past
* We carry emotional scars
* Emotional triggers surface
* Triggers are part of the process
* The journey is endless

CHAPTER 13

Elements of Our Thinking and Feeling Nature

TO BEGIN WITH, let's take a survey of essential elements of our inner being, all alive in the Emotional part. The elements are: consciousness, thought, emotion, feeling, and ego. **SECRET.** *What goes on internally is shown externally in our affairs, our own life experiences, our eating habits, our weight.* What we think of our bodies, what kinds of food and how much food we eat, and every other thing we can imagine, happens inside first, in our Mental/Emotional Being.

ELEMENT 1. Consciousness, Awareness
Anything and everything a conscious person or group has ever thought, felt, known, or perceived, from all life's experiences.

ELEMENT 2. Volition
The ability to control one's own action by choice. We will use Mind and Consciousness as synonyms.

Knowing and putting the word *choice* into a working modality in our lives is power. **SECRET.** *When we know and practice being at choice, our lives will change instantly.* You don't have to eat the entire bag of cookies. You can get up, wipe the cookie crumbs off your face, and do something else. You now have tools, techniques and information to use. What you did a moment ago has nothing to do with what your next move will be. You can make another choice.

ELEMENT 3. Thought

Thought is a movement in consciousness, the process of thinking. It is the ability to understand and form ideas. Reasoning, judging and imagining. Just as you can choose your behavior, you can also choose your thoughts. In the Mental part, you were taught a visualization exercise, picturing yourself in front of the mirror. You imagine your new being into reality; this is a version of choosing your thoughts. Those were and continue to be as often as you do that exercise, purposeful thoughts. You choose to say affirmations, positive statements about yourself. You are making these a part of your day's mental activities. You are powerful and making smart choices. Your are exercising your mind. You are transforming.

What if you've sunk in the depths of negative thoughts, swirling and whirling around in your mind? Your energy is low and you have been in a low spot for some time. You are emotionally low. **SECRET.** *Now you can see that you put yourself there by the choices you made about the thoughts you let follow their course.* You can get yourself out of that negative place by choosing to think positively instead. The best news is that you're not using food to stuff the thoughts and feelings. You're making great progress.

So how can you get from a downer thought to a higher thought, as quickly as possible? First, you have to be aware of the thought. When the urge to consume the refrigerator hits, Halt, and ask yourself what you're feeling and thinking. Use the urge to eat as a signal that something else is going on. You are likely thinking negative thoughts of some kind, about your body, about your weight, about your life or relationships, for example. It might take some time to figure out what those thoughts are, and find the feelings underlying the urge to eat, and it might be uncomfortable to face them, but each day you practice, you become healthier. Food is not your problem. **SECRET.** *Food is what you're using to try to fix what's wrong.*

Here are some more simple suggestions. If you have tendencies to play the victim role, you may have to give yourself a swift kick to get this exercise going. Any time of the day, wherever you are when you're in a funk, stop. Stop eating, stop fretting, stop worrying. For just a moment, think of something that makes you feel better. It can be as simple as a memory of a family member, a beautiful sunset. It doesn't matter. Grab that thought, then think of another one. Then another. Continue on and on until you're out of the funk. You can't stay down thinking of something good that makes you feel better. It's impossible. How you get from a downer thought to a higher thought, and what you do with those downer thoughts coming through on a positive side is self-mastery.

SECRET. *Exercise is great for altering moods.* Sometimes if I am in a low mood, I put music on and move. Music immediately changes my mood and I feel better instantly, and dancing gets my blood moving. Remember your tools, talking it out with someone, your journal, Halt. Give yourself pleasure, not pain. Pleasure of course. Get into the habit of giving yourself a power surge of positive feelings, positive thoughts, and affirmations.

ELEMENT 4. Emotions

Emotions and feelings are synonyms in dictionaries and are used interchangeably when we communicate. However, there is a difference. An emotion is a reaction or response to a specific stimuli; it is felt physically and experienced mentally. Feelings are sensitiveness, or the capacity to feel deeply. I'll use them synonymously since they may be confusing. They confuse me at times.

Often how you perceive stimuli will determine your emotional response. If you attend a party and saunter over to the dessert table, you'll likely have an emotional reaction to all the beauties presenting themselves to you. You might be triggered to feel not only pleasure at the sight, but fear of eating them all, or despair, knowing that even though you don't eat them there, you'll stop on the way home and buy ten. You might feel sad knowing you can't eat them all. But wait, that was the old you. You can now look at the little beauties and appreciate them, feel happiness that you are able to choose a few, and not go back for more. Enjoy.

If you have a disagreement with someone and tension mounts and you feel your face getting warm and your hands perspiring, you know you are angry. You can choose to lash out with angry words or you can choose another response. You can breathe slowly, very slowly. Without raging or raising your voice, you can talk in a normal tone, and talk slowly. You can make a conscious decision not to react. You can state your case calmly. It's that simple.

Remember boundaries? This is a good example of you setting the boundaries over which you'll not step. You choose to remain calm, and not let the other person's actions affect you. You'll be in the power seat and the other person will be put off balance by your calmness. Anger is a natural reaction but what we do with it becomes a choice. Women especially have been taught and conditioned to stifle it, to stuff it, to eat. You know better now. Choosing to react differently will produce a feeling of calm. You will walk away from that experience feeling grown up. That is a true gift, walking away not feeling like a frightened five year old. And now you know that if you've done it once you can do it again.

Perhaps you are thinking that I haven't been addressing food. I have been, it's been subtle. These are the underlying issues that drive us to being out of control with food. I believe it's most important to get the food issues under control in order to deal with the real problems, but it's really the easy part when it comes down to it. If you don't get this information, where the true healing lives, you may be back to thinking that food is your problem again when it isn't.

You may have to remind yourself of that from time to time, so it can truly be understood and absorbed. Be open and ready to receive. You've come so far now. Perhaps you've tried many times in the past without permanent results but if you practice, practice, practice your new skills and techniques, you'll be amazed at the new you. Practice and patience.

You can apply all of the skills presented here to life and living, and begin to live life in a lighter, happier new way. I've heard that life is a treasure hunt to bliss. You're on the hunt now and you're finding one treasure after another. From understanding, to new skills, to new behavior, to freedom around food, those are all moments of bliss. More are on the way.

Sometimes our feelings carry us through life, and we act and react to them without truly knowing what they are, or what we're doing. How many times have you asked yourself: "What did I just eat and why?" Have you let your emotions carry you through life as I did? When we begin to be open and become aware, we can choose different responses. One of the problems is that food is great for calming our fears, stifling anger, and it really can control emotions but in reality we know it's only temporarily. It doesn't solve anything, doesn't fix anything, and usually only adds pounds to the hips. We cry, scream, eat, pout, go silent, get angry, get happy, eat, blame but wait a moment. That was in the past, right? No longer will those feelings churn around and around in your mind and show up on your hips. We are skilled at dealing with the challenges that now come to us.

You're really beginning to take care of yourself now. You're learning to deal with life on new terms, and how to walk away from people, places, and things you no longer need. You're dealing with your emotions and the excessive foods, and the foods that aren't good for you. You're taking care of your needs. Think of all the emotions we have, from one extreme to the other. Perhaps, if we named them, and narrowed them down, they would fall under two categories, positive and negative.

ELEMENT 5. Ego

The self. You. The awareness of yourself. Your thoughts defining yourself, positive and negative.

My ego used to be terribly bruised, all the time. I was extremely sensitive, or so I thought. I had a classic case of overreacting to just about everything. If someone looked at me wrong, I cried or went silent. I took everything personally. My feelings got hurt over nothing, or I imagined all kinds of scenarios. Of course I stuffed all the hurt feelings down, down, down, with food. Do you stuff to push the feelings down? Not any longer as you're learning healthy ways to get your feelings out.

One of my problems was expecting life to be good and happy all the time. Life isn't like that. It's not going to be fair sometimes. Sometimes we lose when we think we should win. We experience wins and successes, many in the course of a day. Remember, life happens. Your choice involves which of those to focus on, and how to respond. You can have freedom and peace of mind. Practice, practice, practice. In a split second, we can change from tears to laughter. Would you consider that self-mastery?

Because we know we can select our thoughts, and our feelings come from our thoughts, we can just as easily select our feelings as well. We know now we are responsible; our earlier experiences don't determine our actions, feelings or thoughts of today. Remember, since we have the power to change our thought at any given time, we can experience another feeling. There's much power in knowing we're at choice.

SECRET. *You have the power to choose something new at any given moment.*

REMEMBER

* You are a thinking, feeling being
* You are choosing every moment
* Exercise alters moods
* We react emotionally to life
* Healthy egos are good

CHAPTER 14

Wisdom From the Teachers

❤

IN HIS BOOK, *You'll see it when you believe it*, Wayne Dyer tells us that "If the results continually are that you do not lose weight, get to work to discover the belief system that is keeping you fat, because it is your thoughts that are creating the unwanted results. The most effective methods for doing this in my opinion, are in the programs which emphasize that you have your own answers. Find the approach that suits you, an approach involving self-responsibility and understand that what you believe is what you see".

Jamie Sams speaks of those same choices in his work titled "Earth Medicine":
The promise Creator gives us
Comes with every new day,
The gift of breath, the gift of life,
Opportunities in a vast array.
How do we count our blessings,
Through the choices life can bring?
Is it through joyful lessons?
Or the fears to which we cling?
Are we learning to show gratitude,
For the victories over human pain?
By honoring the feeling choices,
We grasp the will we've regained.
Can we change our focus,
With no need to defend?

Acknowledging joy and sorrow,
Without judging foe or friend?
Tomorrow promises the fullness
Of every human way to know:
How we master each challenge
Determines our balance.

Stephen Covey tells us to remember: "Response-ability is the ability to choose our response to any circumstance or condition. When we are response-able, our commitment becomes more powerful than our moods or circumstances, and we keep the promises and resolutions we make…and gain a certain sense of self-mastery." From Principle-centered Leadership. (Covey, 71).

When you have a setback and realistically you will because that is part of the process, you may want to go back and read the above. You have the power in every situation. When I first began to get a grasp of the concept that everything was a choice, it was hard, foreign. I found it difficult because the habit of crisis and chaos was ingrained in my mind. It took time, and I'm still practicing. Writing this book has given me the opportunity to look at my own reactions to people. Yes, I still do react negatively at times but not as blind as I did in the past. And never do I seek food for consolation. You won't either.

REMEMBER

*   We are responsible to ourselves
*   You have your own answers
*   Choose healthy responses

CHAPTER 15

How Not to React

ONE OF THE MOST RECENT examples of me not choosing my reactions and instead letting circumstances determine my behavior, what I felt, was when I put money down on a house. The seller refused to refund my earnest money when I chose not to buy. After an episode in small claims court in which he lied to keep from paying me, the old me took over and I became a living reactive machine. It was as if I had never learned any of the things in this book. I was rude and mean to the man, I spoke faster than I thought I could talk, and didn't recognize myself in anything I said. The judge's eyes crossed as I finished and stalked out.

As I drove away, I realized I could've chosen a different response. I might have instead simply not reacted. No response can be an appropriate response. Or I could have calmly stated my case. Unfortunately, my reaction was inappropriate and overly emotional. While I was proud that I had stood up for myself, I could have found a much more mature and sensible way to do so. The next time I will prepare myself and choose different behavior. Life happens.

Additionally, who knows what the seller was going through at the time. Maybe his past experiences triggered him as well. We all have our own stories, and understanding that is essential.

The great news: In the past, I would have driven immediately to the grocery store and purchased many of my favorite foods. I would've opened the packages before I got to the checkout counter, and eaten most of the food before I got home. That courtroom event would have been an excuse to continue eating throughout the evening. Probably that binge would have walked into the next day and many days to follow. I would've chosen isolation plus food and I would never have traced it back to old emotional scars.

This time, I never considered doing any of that. That's freedom! I did, however, remain in a hissy fit until I got to the phone and talked it over with a several of my friends. I got the good out of it, the realizations about the source of my behavior, and was able to release the whole event. Many times, encounters that cause us to react actually have nothing to do with the present. **SECRET.** *Pay attention to your reactions, and see if you can find those old emotional scars.* They don't even have to be huge or traumatic. They just have to have happened. Remember: "I let go of things that no longer serve me".

REMEMBER

* No response is a response
* Pay attention to your reactions
* React consciously

CHAPTER 16

Healing Techniques From the Experts

HAVE YOU HEARD the old saying: "no pain, no gain?" We don't need to be in pain to grow. That's also a choice. We can grow and evolve without being a wreck and I'm going to show you how.

Everyone is driven by core issues, deep seated beliefs and emotions. What follows is information from experts in the field of Imago Therapy, EMDR, Sexual abuse and Emotional Freedom Technique. Imago Therapy is Relationship Therapy and explains how relationships can stimulate food issues and more. EMDR helps to neutralize the toxic effects of stressful traumatic events in one's life. A section on Sexual abuse and Emotional Freedom Technique have been added. With the process of EFT, you will learn how to gently tap on meridian points to help the body process negative energy and release it. These processes and techniques are presented to help you move past the subconscious reactions your might not be aware of. Destructive emotions such as fear, anger, guilt, and in my opinion the most damaging, shame which can be released by these processes.

The food cycle can start in a number of ways. Sometimes, we can become so consumed by negative emotions that our moments of living become dull and lifeless. Food looks especially good at these times and the more we eat the more guilt and shame we feel. This is the ugly cycle. Emotions are triggers. The more we wallow in them, the more control they can have. Make a choice to move past them.

Remember, thinking of something that makes you happy, even a tiny moment will get you moving forward.

One of the strongest driving forces, the causes, of these emotions is our relationships. We spend our lives in relationships of many kinds and they can induce intense emotions and can trigger our food issues. We get married and sometimes divorce. We may have affairs or someone else does, or we lose a spouse or friend to illness or anger. We eat over the losses and confusion. But that was then and this is now. We're learning to make other choices.

Imago Therapy

I want to introduce Imago Relationship Therapy, and Eye Movement Desensitization Reprocessing, EMDR as important therapeutic processes that increase the discovery and insight phases of therapy. Imago therapy helped me uncover many buried issues from the past and EMDR provided a concrete way for healing many emotions. Both the Imago work and EMDR helped me get to the heart of what was driving my emotional energy from my past, so that I could redirect myself into a more positive future. If you experience fear and other unpleasant emotions you don't understand, you may want to explore these techniques.

Saundra Dickinson, a Licensed Marriage & Family Therapist in Houston, Texas, wrote an insert for my book, and now you have the opportunity to have firsthand information for both Imago Therapy and EMDR.

Saundra has served on the board of Imago Relationships International with Harville Hendrix Ph.D., the founder of Imago Therapy, and she offers many books and CD's on these subjects. She can be reached at 281-358-3299, and her website is: www.saundradickinson.com. If you wanted to pursue Imago or EMDR, you could also contact a local therapist in your area.

For you from Saundra Dickinson

You might be wondering why Linda asked me to discuss Imago Relationship Therapy and EMDR in a book about food issues. The answer is simple, though it may feel elusive at first. Unhealthy relationships can trigger food issues. Unhealthy emotions feed food issues just like unhealthy emotions keep people stuck in unhealthy relationships. The following information goes beyond developing healthy relationships with food, it is about developing healthy relationships with each other. Emotions are triggered as we relate to others. Food is a way to avoid working on those emotions that surface in relationships. Imago Therapy and EMDR Therapy are two ways to access unresolved pain from our early conditioning. It's in this pain that the negative messages and emotions about ourselves from those early, vulnerable experiences are held, and that will most likely set into motion a pattern of self-defeating behaviors (addictive behaviors). All addictive behaviors become self-defeating to the individual who uses them.

Imago Relationship Therapy was co-created and introduced by Harville Hendrix, Ph.D.,and Helen Kelly Hunt, Ph.D., in their groundbreaking book, *Getting The Love You Want* in 1989. Imago Theory is a complex, multi-faceted theory developed to help all of us understand what actually happens when two people meet, fall in love, make a life-long commitment to each other, get married, and then over 50% of the time, end up divorced. Imago Relationship Theory helps to clarify what happens when we fall in and out of love, and explores what conflict in our relationships is trying to achieve. It offers insights into the unconscious agenda each partner brings to their relationships, and it provides a way to bring this hidden agenda into the open so that we can see and understand the disparity between each partner's goals, hopes, and expectations of each other. With this information and insight, we can begin to cooperate with this hidden agenda and discover the new possibilities of relationship. As a result, we grow together in a creative, connected, and healing way that creates a more loving, passionate, safe, fun-filled, and intimate relationship.

Some of the main Imago concepts include:

· Romantic Love, the 1st stage of a Primary Love Relationship, connects us with someone who has traits that are similar to specific positive and negative traits in our parents/caretakers. We are aware of these positive traits during Romantic Love and are drawn to them within our love partner.

· The unconscious purpose of Romantic Love is to finish childhood by establishing a bond with another person whom we feel can and will meet needs that were not met in childhood. What remains unfinished in all of us is unconscious to us during Romantic Love, and we are unwilling to be aware of negative traits of our love partner in Romantic Love. But our unfinished business from childhood will become evident to us during the 2nd stage of a Primary Love Relationship, the Power Struggle, in the form of negative, frustrating behaviors of our love partner.

· The fading of romance and the appearance of conflict that usher in the Power Struggle are natural progressions in all relationships. Conflict is viewed as not only inevitable, but necessary. For buried within the frustrations of each partner lies the information necessary for the growth and healing of each partner and the marriage.

· But Romantic Love and the Power Struggle are transient states, and they end when both partners discover the path to Real Love. When we understand that we have chosen our partners to heal certain wounds, and that the healing of those wounds is the key to the end of longing (unrequited love), we have taken the first step on the journey to Real Love.

· By listening with empathy to each other's cues and needs, partners learn how to heal each other's childhood wounds and invite a connected love into the "sacred space between" in their lives.

Imago Theory does not believe our parents were horrible people. In fact, we know that whatever our parents did, they did the best they knew to do at the time, and of course, most of our parents were raised by people who didn't know much more about raising children than their own parents did, and so on and so on. Needless to say, most of us were hurt enough as children to fear trusting anyone long term. And that was also true of our parents and their parents and so on, as far back as we want to go. We do not look for excuses or blame in using Imago Theory. We are solution-oriented and work to help couples gain the insight necessary to grow up emotionally and heal each other in marriage and learn the skills and tools needed for a long-term, committed love relationship.

In the most simple terms possible, Imago Theory is guided by the belief that we survive our childhood in whatever ways possible, grow up enough to leave home, become attracted to a person who has just the right amount of the positive and negative traits of our primary caretakers, marry that person, then realize that our partner for life is completely incompatible with us, and the life-long commitment of marriage was a horrible mistake. At that point, we Americans usually get divorced at least 50+ % of first marriages. Then, we will become attracted to another person who appears to be the opposite of our former partner, but who can eventually cause us to feel the same deadly pain we felt with our first spouse because the pain is inside each of us from childhood, and of course we carry our pain with us because we carry our histories with us wherever we go and with whomever we attach. As long as we are not committed in a relationship, this pain remains somewhat dormant, and we are usually not very aware of it. The wounding that caused us the greatest pain as children will not get triggered unless we get into a committed love relationship with a partner. All of this proves to be true because our choices for a mate are unconscious, based on the unresolved, unseen pains we endured and survived as a child. This cycle will continue until at least one or preferably both partners can hold the tension of their discomfort long enough to begin the process of learning the necessary skills and gain some insight into the growth that is trying to happen in their marriage.

Marriage is an ever-changing energy, moving through very predictable stages that require growth, healing, and new ways of relating to each other. It is crucial that couples understand that the love they professed at the altar will not hold them for a lifetime. When couples do not realize this and the Power Struggle surfaces, they keep doing the same destructive behaviors within their marriage until it is almost or completely destroyed. Understanding that your marriage is going to move through developmental stages whether you and your partner are aboard or not, just as surely as you moved through physical, intellectual, and emotional developmental stages as a child whether you knew it or not, or whether you received any help with that growth or not, can make all the difference in this world to the quality of your marriage. Imago Therapy provides this information along with the tools to put this new knowledge into action.

EMDR Healing past experiences that effect our present

It is a powerful, rather new method, since the mid 1980's. EMDR is used in psychotherapy to help a person work on the present-day impact of experiences from the past that intrude into one's life. It is based on the discovery that the body's natural process of rapid eye movement sleep patterns seems to somehow be connected with the brain's ability to process negative material. It was discovered by Dr. Francine Shapiro as she began to make a connection between eye movement under certain conditions and the reduction of disturbing thoughts. Dr. Shapiro continued her studies around this phenomenon and in 1989 reported significant success in treating victims of trauma in the Journal of Traumatic Stress. Since then, EMDR has developed and evolved into a set of protocols that are used worldwide by over 30,000 trained EMDR therapists.

We know that when a person is very upset or experiences prolonged stress, his or her brain cannot process information as it does ordinarily. A disturbing experience or the perception of a negative experience can be recorded in the body and brain, but left unprocessed. Typically, we develop negative beliefs about ourselves in relation to these types of disturbing events and perceptions, for example, being obsessive about food. Such memories can have a lasting negative effect on the way a person sees the world and relates to other people that interfere with his or her life. Using EMDR consistently demonstrates that the negative energy surrounding stressful or traumatic events in a person's life becomes less disturbing, allowing one to become unstuck and move on in a more positive way with their life.

Following an EMDR session using the eight-step protocol with an EMDR trained therapist and client, the images, sounds, and feelings of a disturbing event or belief are still remembered; however, the degree of distressful emotions has often significantly lessened. Follow-up studies confirm that the results of EMDR are highly effective and long lasting. It has been established by substantial scientific research that EMDR is effective for treating post traumatic stress. It has also been reported by clinicians to be very effective in treating Depression, Anxiety, Panic Attacks, OCD (Obsessive Compulsive Disorder), Addictions, Trauma, including Post Traumatic Stress Disorder, Dissociative Disorders, Disturbing Memories, Phobias, Stress Reduction, Performance Anxiety, Complicated Grief, Sexual and/or Physical Abuse.

As EMDR has evolved, various ways have been developed by clinicians to bilaterally stimulate the brain from eye movement to ear phones to tactile methods of tapping the knees, shoulders, or hands. Therapists have discovered that it is the rhythmic, back and forth stimulation of the right and left hemispheres of the brain that seems to stimulate something we call the *information processing system* to go into a highly accelerated mode of functioning, which is exactly the treatment effect we must create to get the results we want. EMDR helps us process the negative energy surrounding the negative beliefs that remain unprocessed in our brain and body and keep us stuck in our life.

Just as a laugh is the body's way of getting involved in our ability to process positive material, bilateral stimulation under certain conditions seems to be the body's way of getting involved in helping us neutralize the high degree of distressful emotions surrounding a previous disturbing event or series of events in our life.

More published case reports and controlled outcome research supports EMDR than any other method used in treatment of Post Traumatic Stress Disorder. Since the initial efficacy study (Shapiro, 1898a), positive therapeutic results with EMDR have been reported and studied with a wide range of populations. "A study comparing the effectiveness of Prozac vs. EMDR showed that EMDR was more successful than Prozac in achieving substantial and sustained reductions in anxiety and depression," The Journal of Clinical Psychiatry, January 2007.

The website of the EMDR Institute in California (www.emdr. com) contains information on a multitude of studies and ongoing work in EMDR. References and a bibliography of research on EMDR may be obtained through the institute, as well as a list of EMDR-trained therapists in your area. Recommended reading: EMDR, The Breakthrough Therapy by Francine Shapiro, Ph.D. and Margot Silk Forest.

These two therapeutic processes, Imago Relationship Therapy and EMDR, seem like a natural combination and blend seamlessly together. EMDR works on helping neutralize the toxic effects of stressful/traumatic events, experiences, and perceptions that have occurred in one's life, and Imago is based on the belief that the damage, negative beliefs, we bring into our adult relationships, especially our marriage, is unconscious to us, yet crippling to our lives with those whom we want to be close. One seems to solve the other. If we can discover the negative beliefs we operate under, we can understand more clearly the healing needed in our relationships. Plus, we will gain a new respect for ourselves and our partner and understand our struggles so much more clearly and avoid the judgment and condemnation that can arise without this knowledge.

My experience with EMDR

As a youngster, I dreamed of becoming an actor and a dancer as I mentioned early in my book. I went to college and earned a BS in Physical Education with a minor in Speech and Drama. Finally, as an adult, I was recommitting and had registered for an acting class. However, to my surprise, I encountered huge blocks being in class. I felt tremendous shame being in front of people, shame that seemed to have no source. It was difficult to concentrate and be present. The more I got up the worse it got for me. As much as I wanted to learn, I was stuck and couldn't make progress. As much as I wanted to attend class, I disliked it just as much. My actions and thoughts contradicted one another.

What was going on? In the past, I had no power over food and now I was experiencing the same feeling of powerlessness in this class. But, I had my food issues resolved. Didn't I? Shouldn't life be easy and smooth? It was clear the problem wasn't food, but what was it? We are always unfolding and growing into new levels of understanding and healing, and once I thought about it enough, I was ready to take the next step. I was ready to look at this ugly in the eye.

I began my sessions with Saundra and she immediately took me back to the sixth grade. I had a cruel teacher who got pleasure in putting down the students. After tests, she called out the grades from 100 on down the scale, and as she called them out, each student stood. I was always near the bottom, reinforcing the feeling of being stupid my first grade teacher had instilled in me.

It became very clear to me as I was doing the EMDR session that the feelings I was experiencing in my acting class were the same ones I had experienced in school. Today, when I get in a classroom situation, I sometimes slip back into the sixth grade but I don't have the huge emotional charge that I once had. But at times I do have some energy over it. Now I understand it's old "stuff". It's not as traumatic as it once was and now I have tools to address it. Healing continues.

If you have violent memories and can't get them out of your mind, or simply reactions to situations that don't seem appropriate, you may want to consider EMDR. EMDR is a powerful tool that can help uncover the pain, and then heal it.

Healing the hurt that runs your life

I experienced another wonderful person on my path, Bill Ferguson, also in Houston, Texas. Bill is an ex-divorce attorney turned healer and consultant. Bill's work has been featured on Oprah, and he has many books, workbooks, CD's, and cassettes available. He was also open to contributing information for my book. If you want more information about Bill and his technique, he can be reached at 713-520-5370 for a private phone consultation. You can find him on the internet at: www.masteryoflife.com and billferguson.com.

It was long after I became free of food issues that I came in contact with him, and I thought I had it all figured out once again. During one of his workshops, "Return to the Heart," I experienced another aha moment that took me by surprise and was very revealing. It was similar to the revelation I had about feeling dumb and stupid.

His instructions were to close our eyes and he would call out a word for each letter of the alphabet. He told us that one word would affect us more than any other. As he got close to the end of the alphabet my thought was that I was so together, none of the words jumped out at me. Surprise, surprise. The word that got me, "unwor-thy." Suddenly, my gut was on fire and my heart felt as if it was going to pop out of my body. I've done a lot of healing around the idea of not being worthy. "Unworthy" seems to be a universal belief. Not too long ago I discovered another, "unwanted". The surprises keep coming and the healing also. Personally, I like the ideas of worthy, wanted, desirable, lovable, fantastic and on and on and on.

For you from Bill Ferguson

The technique that follows was very helpful to me and perhaps will be for you also, if you choose to try. I've practiced it quite often. Here it is: When you were a young child, you were pure love. You were happy, alive and free. But you were born into a world that suppresses this state. As a result, you got hurt, and you got hurt a lot. As a little child, the only way you could explain these painful losses of love was to blame yourself. In a moment of hurt, you created the belief that you were worthless, not good enough, a failure, not worth loving or in some other way not okay.

This wasn't the truth, but to a little child, this was the only ex-planation that made any sense at the time. You then fought the very notion that you created. "No one can ever love me if I'm worthless. Worthless is a horrible way to be."

The moment you decided that you were not okay, you created a mechanism, or core issue, that would then sabotage the rest of your life. From that moment on, the underlying focus of your life would be to avoid this hurt. Unfortunately, everything you do to avoid this hurt creates more of it. If you are running from failure, you will create a life of failure. If you are running from worthless, you will create more worthless. By fighting this belief, you give it power and magnify it out of proportion.

Fortunately, it is possible to heal this hurt. The first step is to find what the hurt is. To do this, make a list of all the major upsets you have had in our life. Find at least twelve. Then go to the hurt that is under each hurt and ask yourself this question: "According to the hurt, what do those circumstances say about me?"

If someone left you and this was painful, this might say that you are not worth loving. If you get fired from a job, this might say that you are a failure or not good enough. Look for the words of "not okay" that hurt the most. Remember, you are not looking for the truth. You are looking for the suppressed emotion. The more painful the words, the closer you are to your hurt. As you work with your upsets, you will notice that the same hurt keeps showing up, over and over. This is the hurt that runs your life.

After you find your hurt, the next step is to take away its power. You do this by facing the dragon and owning this part of you. This is not part of you in reality, but it is very real in your reality. You have just been fighting it.

To heal this hurt, you have to do the opposite of what gives it power. Instead of fighting and denying this part of you, own it and make peace with it. As you do this, the hurt loses power and can eventually disappear.

To face the dragon there are several steps to take. The first is to put yourself in the hurt of feeling worthless or whatever your issue is. Then look into your life and see all the evidence to prove that this is indeed part of you.

The opposite is also true. You are also very worthy, but the worthy side of the coin isn't causing any problems. So go back to the side of the coin that you have been avoiding and let in how truly worthless you really are. Then dive into the hurt of feeling this way. Cry as hard as you can. Cry because you want to reach in, grab it, and pull it out. If there aren't any tears, fake the tears. Get this suppressed hurt out of you.

Let the fact in that you are this way and gently move to the place of "So what?" As you face the dragon and own this part of you, you will discover that the dragon is just an illusion and has no teeth. This discovery will then change the rest of your life. You will be more able to flow with life and more able to have your dreams come true.

With those words he presents us with another technique to uncover lots of hidden treasures. That is an interesting way of looking at it. Freedom is now yours. When we become conscious of our thoughts, we can then manage our feelings in a more positive way. We can choose our responses rather than become five years old. The five-year-old will fade away and the new you will be operating on a much different level. Your self-confidence continues to soar.

Sexual Abuse: Recognize and recover from the trauma

Many individuals who are obese may have been sexually abused. Many of them don't know what to do to heal. Food becomes important as it's an easily available tool to cover up unresolved shame, fear, guilt and anger. And from the foods come layers and layers of unwanted pounds to protect their wounded past. I have included a short section on sexual abuse and food written by Dell deBerardinis, I hope it helps. If it doesn't resonate with you, please feel free to move on to the next chapter.

Sexual Abuse: Recognition and recovery

My colleague, Linda Martin has produced this incredible book in response to the needs of thousands of individuals who struggle with eating issues and food. Her story is a powerful lesson in what is possible with someone who finds themselves unable to control food and weight. There are many avenues to weight loss, diets, exercise plans, etc. What Ms. Martin knows is that it takes much more than a diet to fix eating issues. She has proven it by living it and is now able to help others.

What Ms. Martin recognizes is an old adage that I repeat to my counseling clients often: it is not always what we eat but what is eating us. The underlying factors and causes of eating issues are many. I am a therapist that specializes in trauma and abuse issues and have discovered that my clients who suffer from food and eating issues more likely than not have some traumatic past that is contributing to their inability to manage their bodies and food. The misuse of food like any other addictive behavior generally has underlying components.

If the food struggle is never-ending, if you have dieted many years in yo-yo fashion and cannot seem to keep the weight off, if your body image is not something you are proud of, then perhaps this information is for you.

Some of the material included in this section may not be applicable to you but if you find that it is and need more information or have questions feel free to contact me at 281-363-2060 or email me at doseofdell@gmail.com. I am the author of a more complete guide to sexual abuse recovery called Sexual Abuse: Recognition and Recovery. You can get your copy by contacting my office. What follows is a brief overview.

Trauma and abuse recognition and definition
With all family trauma and abuse issues there are what I call set-ups, symptoms, and solutions. The set-ups are the actual abusive acts toward a child that are sometimes overt and sometimes covert. The symptoms are the long-term effects these acts have on a child, often carrying into adulthood and reflected in chronic behavioral patterns such as overeating, under-eating and/or general body image problems.

Sexual abuse
Sexual abuse is a set-up for many problems related to food and eating issues. It impairs the development of a healthy ego and many times results in inappropriate sexual behavior, negative body image,

sexual acting out or the reverse which I call sexual anorexia. This can carry into food anorexia as well.

Overt abuse

Sexually abusive behaviors occur in the form of both overt and covert behaviors. The overt behaviors lend themselves to the legal description rather than the clinical description of abuse. These behaviors relate to sexualized touching such as fondling, penetration, oral and anal sex, and kissing.

Covert abuse

The covert abuses are often less physically intrusive but are not less damaging. Many victims I have worked with have experienced verbal sexual assaults, name calling, exposure to pornography, voyeuristic acts, and/or exposure to inappropriate nudity. The covert abuses include voyeuristic and exhibitionistic behaviors. A typical example of survivors I have worked with are feelings of being stared at or looked at in an invasive way, while others report having had holes drilled in the walls of bathrooms where someone was watching toilet activity. Visual violations happen with children as well as in the workplace with adults in the form of sexual harassment. Survivors of this type of abuse often minimize its effects not thinking it is actual sexual abuse.

Emotional Incest

A more subtle form of covert abuse is emotional incest or the misuse of children by a caregiver or parent for meeting their own emotional needs. An emotionally immature parent might enmesh a child, placing them in the role of a spouse or parent. This emotional intrusion is heavily correlated with over eating. When children are pulled into the role of meeting the emotional needs of the parent, it is a setup for a variety of obsessive behaviors especially over-eating and sexual acting out.

Behaviors associated with sexual abuse

Anxiety disorders: Terror is a feeling associated with abuse especially of the body. An anxiety attack is set off by terror. The emotion of terror may have abuse as its source.

Depression: Most survivors will experience bouts of mild to serious depression at some time in their history. When we discuss the profound loneliness and isolation the survivor has experienced at the moment of the abuse, it is easy to see how the feelings of despair and hopelessness may still be present.

Somatic disorders: Somatic refers to the body's memory of past experiences. Many times the body remembers what the mind doesn't. It does not forget that it has been abused and survivors may be plagued with somatic complaints, high stress-related diseases, problems with genitals, urinary tract, headaches, bowel or colon dysfunction, or ulcers. Eating disorder and food issues are closely related to other somatic complaints.

Compulsions and addictive behaviors

Repetitive addictive behaviors are extremely prevalent in survivors of sexual abuse. Ninety percent of adolescent females admitted to chemical dependency units report sexual abuse in their history. The correlation of addiction and abuse is obvious when recognizing the survivors need to survive and find ways to cope with the pain of abuse.

Eating disorders, food and body issues

Eating disorders are extremely complicated and are not always associated with childhood sexual abuse. However, experts suggest that 65 to 75 percent of individuals with compulsivity around food have sexual abuse in their history.

Anorexia: Anorexic behavior has a number of characteristics common to abuse survivors. The first is the issue of control. Many survivors experience a feeling of lack of control over their own destiny and behaviorally will control the body's image and intake, the only thing they can control. Another dynamic of underlying sexual abuse is the unconscious need to disappear or to not exist. This may sound strange but if you are an under-eater you will understand this need to not exist. It appears to represent a feeling of worthlessness or is an attempt to protect the child from further abuse through nonexistence. Anorexics feel betrayed by their bodies. Starvation is an unconscious effort to get rid of the body.

Bulimia: My experience has taught me that bulimia can often be associated with incidences of oral sexual abuse. It is difficult to separate and define the various eating disorders as many individuals vacillate between all of the behaviors. The survivors attempt to control one behavior may result in acting out in another.

Compulsive overeating: Compulsive overeating can be an attempt to hide the underlying pain associated with sexual abuse both overt and covert. Many dynamics associated with anorexic behavior, especially those related to control issues, may also be true for a compulsive overeater. Overeating is comforting and can be the unconscious effort on the child's part to wrap themselves with protection. Eating disorders are often present when physical sexual abuse is not but emotional incest is.

In working with survivors and their addictive propensities, I have found a12-step program to be very helpful in managing compulsivity.

Again, please check Appendix A for more information about abuse.

Emotional freedom technique

By now you understand how we can be driven by our past in ways that rob us of our freedom, and don't allow us to express who we are and what we want to do and be. We are driven on a subconscious level until the time in our awakening when we intuitively know it's time to get unstuck. No time to waste. What a grand thought. Every day is a new adventure in learning about yourself. Treasure it.

Delving deeper now, you're going to be given a technique that will zoom into the problems of food issues and zap the negative in a very specific way. I had the honor of meeting Beverly Nadler in Vancouver, Canada at a T. Harv Eker workshop a couple of years ago. If you don't know about T. Harv Eker, you may want to look him up on the internet. In my opinion, he's the ultimate in presenters. He doesn't address food issues but helps people transform their lives in countless ways. He has awesome programs related to personal growth.

Back to Beverly. You know how you hit it off with someone and conversation takes off. That's what happened with Beverly and me. Before I knew it, I had in my hands a jewel of a book that she had written, *Vibrational Harmony*. www.vibrationalharmonybook.com. It was my first introduction to Emotional Freedom Techniques. EFT was first developed by Gary Graig. Beverly has refined some of the techniques and put them into her own words. She notes him in her book.

If you saw the popular movie, *The Secret* you saw Dr. John F. Demartini's presentation. Here are some inserts from the introduction Dr. Demartini wrote in Beverly Nadler's book: "Her teachings and writings have led and challenged me to ever greater vision and action. Her dedicated study of the laws of the universe, as they relate to self-mastery, are signs of her commitment to humanity. She has found the philosopher's stone, the essence, the elixir, the principles that will stand the tests of time, those mysterious truths that awaken greatness, and help make immortals out of mortals. Her special new book entitled *Vibrational Harmony* is a gem that glimmers with insight, sparkles with beauty and sizzles with wisdom We are all here to shine, but we all certainly require some polish. Beverly's wisdom and secrets of self-mastery will buff the rough edges off your present life and let you radiate with new and elevated actions and vibrations. It is simply a must in any serious seeker's personal development library." Dr. John F. Demartini, author of *Count your Blessings - The Healing Power of Gratitude and Love.*

Beverly and I stayed connected and she ended up helping me rid myself of many blocks in my subconscious mind. Again, I went to another wonderful person who helped me and asked if she would write some helpful information for my book. I'm so delighted and appreciative for Beverly's contribution and I know you will be helped.

For you from Beverly Nadler

Congratulations on your decision to achieve your weight goals. If you've read this far, chances are you will do the necessary work involved, and you'll be successful.

I know what it's like to struggle with your weight. My weight issues were not nearly as severe as Linda's, nor was my weight loss as impressive as hers. I lost 25 pounds in 1997. I've kept the weight off, and I also trained myself to love exercise, something I used to avoid like the plague because I disliked it so intensely.

What is impressive is that I used the same techniques to lose weight that I used in 1994 to heal from cancer! My 25 lb. weight gain, in fact, was a direct result of my healing. I had shriveled down to 97 pounds while I was sick, and I guess my body was so happy I was healing, it just kept adding the pounds. At first I went back to my normal weight, for which I was grateful. But, then, to my dismay, the weight gain wouldn't stop, even though I reduced my food intake. For several years I could make no headway. Those extra 25 pounds refused to budge until I finally decided to use the same techniques I had used to heal myself. And lo and behold, they worked! These are the same techniques I will be sharing with you.

Why what I teach is important to you

Linda asked me to write this information for a very specific reason. She knows that what I teach is based on the natural laws that are the foundation for success and healing in every area of our life. When you have this knowledge, you will understand why I use the techniques I use, and why and how they work. That understanding gives you the motivation to use the techniques. And when you use them, you will have the excellent results that I and my clients have.

I teach the rules of the game of life, the Universal and Mental Laws that govern our lives. These natural Laws are based on ancient metaphysical teachings, some of which are: we live in an energy universe that is governed by natural law; everything is energy; humans are energy beings; energy vibrates and is magnetic; the energy of the human mind is powerful and creative; you have a body-mind energy connection through which you can heal and literally change your life.

While all of this was once considered science fiction, it is now confirmed by science including psychology, physics and quantum physics. People who are on a path of personal, professional and/or spiritual growth are familiar with these Laws, but the knowledge was so precious that in ancient times it was only allowed to be taught to those who controlled and ruled common man, royalty and religious, political and military leaders. To teach this to the masses would mean death and few teachers would take the chance. It was kept secret from the public for centuries, until recently.

The Secret – What's it all about

Perhaps you're familiar with the 2006 film, *The Secret*. It became an international phenomenon, especially after it was introduced on the Larry King Show. In February 2007, Oprah Winfrey had two shows regarding the film, and she spoke with a number of the people who appeared in the film. Then in March, Montel Williams talked about the film and showcased one of the authors on his show. No doubt the media coverage will continue.

The film, and later, the book, introduced the public to the Law of Attraction one of the Universal and Mental laws, and to the power of our thoughts. In case you're wondering what's the **SECRET**: *Your thoughts radiate into the Universe, and by the Law of Attraction, you attract and create your life.*

If this is a revolutionary concept to you, as it is to millions of people, let me assure you that the statement is true. It just doesn't go far enough. I have been filling in the gaps and missing links of how the Law of Attraction along with the other Universal and Mental laws operate. I also teach powerful techniques for change. Techniques I will be introducing to you.

Let's begin by re-defining the **SECRET**: *By radiating your mental energy into the universe, you can, by Law of Attraction, attract and create what you want in your life!* And that includes the body you desire and deserve.

Does that sound exciting to you? Of course it does! As your mental energy, which includes more than your thoughts radiate into the universe, your vibrations attract to you whatever you are in resonance, or vibrational harmony, with. That's how you get what you get in life, wanted or unwanted.

Before I continue, let me remind you of something that people who first learn about the power of the mind often forget. It is the importance of taking action. Throughout this book you are learning specific actions and behaviors that are very important to your success. I know you'll do them.

The power of your belief

In order to achieve your weight goals, you must believe it's possible to have the body you want. See yourself with that body, affirm that body is yours, now even before you begin your program. Action, doing something different in relationship to what you want, is one of the things that gives you a reason to believe and to expect the results you desire. I believe you deserve a healthy body that looks and feels great, and weighing what you desire.

Taking action when your mind is convinced you can't have the body you want, or can't continue to do what it takes to lose the weight and keep it off, guarantees failure. And so does lack of action, no matter how skilled you are at seeing and thinking yourself with the body you desire. Belief and taking action are both essential.

Let's look at belief now and what you believe about yourself, your body, food, exercise, the people and circumstances in your life, how you think, feel and ultimately behave. What you believe about yourself, about your body, about food, about exercise, about the people and circumstances in your life, determines how you think, feel and ultimately behave. When I speak of belief, I am not just referring to what you consciously believe, but also to the programmed beliefs that operate at the subconscious level, often without your awareness.

If you are not familiar with the terms subconscious mind, programming and programmed belief, they will be clearer as you continue to read. If you are familiar with these terms, something you read in this chapter may deepen your understanding. There is magic in understanding, for when we truly understand something, we are often able to make decisions and take actions that previously seemed impossible.

Your conscious mind – what you are aware of

When we use the word mind, it is important to know our frames of reference. Psychologists divide the mind into two parts, conscious and subconscious. For our purposes, we'll do the same. The conscious mind is the part that thinks, reasons, chooses, judges and decides. It presents you with what you are aware of, what you notice, what you focus upon, what you give your attention to at any given time.

Impressions come to us through our five senses: sight, hearing, taste, touch, smell. We give meaning to these impressions and make decisions based on those thoughts. Your conscious mind has short term memory. You know what I mean. You walk into a room, scratch your head, and say: "Hmm, why did I come in here?"

Your subconscious mind – storehouse of memory

Your subconscious mind, on the other hand, is the storehouse of memory. Everything you have ever experienced from the moment of your birth or the moment of conception or, as some people believe, the moment your soul began its journey, which could be centuries ago is recorded and stored in your subconscious mind. This includes everything you were aware of at the time it occurred. Most is forgotten and unavailable to your conscious mind including what you were not aware of at the time.

Your subconscious continuously records everything that goes on around you. This includes smells you aren't aware of, sounds you don't hear, other people's conversations that you pay no attention to, vague feelings you don't notice, everything within your peripheral vision and more.

What most of your thoughts really are

Why is it important for you to know that the subconscious is a storehouse of memory? Because most of your thoughts are not thoughts at all; they originate in your subconscious mind as automatic reactions to something that was stimulated in your memory bank. We become aware of that stimulation and we call it a thought. Often we aren't aware of the stimulation, rather we notice a feeling. We feel upset, angry, fearful, doubtful, worried, sad, etc., and we don't even know why. When these automatic reactions come to the surface, we mistake them for thoughts.

Most of the time, these automatic reactions are what vibrate into the universe and create and attract our life. The reason so many people don't have the results they desire is because they don't realize that the so-called thoughts they radiate are really subconscious reactions. And your subconscious and conscious minds are frequently in conflict with each other.

Your mental computer and its programs

Your subconscious mind is your mental computer. It has programs just like your PC. They're called beliefs and habits. Like the programs in your PC, they give directions that determine outcomes. You have programs, beliefs and habits for every area of your life. Just as the results you get in your PC are dependent upon which programs are operating at the time, so the results you get in life are dependent upon which programs are operating in your subconscious.

Here's a simple illustration. Let's say you are running the Quicken program in your computer, and you meant to run Publisher. No matter how much you want to write your book, you can't. You can cry, beg, plead, pray, meditate, wish, promise to be good, become angry, yell, scream, bang on your computer, throw it upside down, destroy it with an ax. But until you change the program in your computer, you will not be able to write your book. Instead, you will get directions related to expenses and taxes.

Fortunately, or unfortunately, that's how programs in your mental computer, your subconscious mind works. As related to weight, how can this be fortunate? Well, the skinny minis who eat what they want and never exercise, and the athletic men and women who look fit and love exercise, and eat more food in one meal than you eat in a week have subconscious programs that work for them. When you get to your desired goal, your new program will continue to work for you.

The unfortunate part, of course, is that most overweight people, perhaps you, take off weight then put it back on, then take it off again, then put it back on. It's a never-ending cycle that keeps the multi-billion dollar weight loss industry assured of ever increasing profits. Most people with weight challenges are programmed at the subconscious level to be overweight, fat, obese, huge, chunky, etc., and no matter what they do, that's the default program in their mental computer. Unless specific measures are taken, they are likely to keep going back to that program. An essential part of your weight loss and maintenance program is to convince your subconscious mind of a new belief system. We do that by reprogramming your subconscious mind.

Reprogramming your subconscious mind

If you are not getting what you want, in this case you want to lose weight and keep it off, and have the motivation to do what it takes to achieve your goal, it means that your subconscious mind is not cooperating with your conscious desires. Since you're reading this book, I know that you consciously want a slimmer, trimmer more attractive body. You can have this, as long as you get agreement from your subconscious mind.

There is a difference between programming and reprogramming. Programming refers to repeating and reinforcing something until it becomes an automatic way of thinking and/or behaving. It is the way you learn new things, the way you learned to read, spell, type, drive, use a computer, play tennis, etc.

As long as what you're learning doesn't conflict with something that's already programmed in your subconscious mind, programming yourself, while it may be tedious and time-consuming, is not difficult.

Reprogramming is another story. Now you are trying to change something already programmed in your subconscious into something different.

Here's an illustration. I'm going to assume you drive a car. If you don't, you can still relate to this example. I'll also assume you learned to drive in the United States. You learned by repeating and reinforcing mental instructions and repeating and reinforcing the physical act of driving. While you must concentrate on driving at first, once driving becomes automatic, it is a program in your subconscious. Most people who want to drive can learn how.

Suppose you go to England and rent a car. Now you have to learn to drive on the left side instead of the right. That switch is not easy because the program related to driving that's already in your subconscious is in conflict with the new program you want to install. And your subconscious resists learning a new way of driving.

What does this have to do with losing weight

You have many conscious and subconscious beliefs, habits, programs, emotions, patterns, thoughts, perceptions, etc. about diet, food, weight, exercise, your level of confidence, and other things that are related to your weight challenge. While you are conscious of some of them, many are likely to be buried in your psyche.

Remember this fact: The subconscious mind always resists change of any kind. Reprogramming yourself to lose weight and keeping it off is challenging because you will come up against programs already in your subconscious mind that conflict with and are in opposition to your goals, and they *resist* being changed. Have you noticed? Nevertheless, you are going to overcome the resistance and reprogram yourself.

Reprogramming categories

There are many different steps you can take to reprogram yourself, but they all fall under these four categories: *Awareness, Releasing, Installing and Integrating.*

Awareness: being aware of what you don't want and what you do want, relative to achieving and maintaining your weight and diet goals.

Some of the negatives, what you don't want might be: *I don't want to be fat, I don't want to wear size 18, I don't want to feel insecure, I don't want to hate exercise, I don't want to binge on sweets, I don't want to use eating to deal with stress, I don't want to hate myself for not sticking to my program, etc.*

Your positives would be the opposites: *I want to be trim and fit, I want to wear a size 8, I want to enjoy exercise, I want to prefer healthy foods, I want to handle stress without food, I want to love myself regardless of what I do or don't do, etc.*

Releasing: consists of two steps, identification and releasing. You first identify the thoughts, beliefs, feelings, patterns, behaviors and habits that are in conflict with what you want. Once identified, you use techniques to release or in computer language, delete them.

Installing: putting new programs of what you want into your subconscious mind. There are numerous ways: visualization, mental imagery, affirmations, self-hypnosis, etc. These have been taught for decades. However, they don't work well as long as opposing programs are operating.

Integrating: repeating and reinforcing your new beliefs, thoughts and behaviors over and over, so that they become part of your daily life.

When you program yourself as differentiated from reprogram yourself, you only have three categories. Releasing is not necessary because there are no opposing programs in your subconscious. The reason reprogramming is difficult and usually doesn't work is because it is vital to release negatives first, and this is almost never done. That's why I'm first teaching you the category of Releasing. Then we'll move onto Installing.

Importance of releasing negatives

I consider *releasing* the most important category for reprogramming.

If you don't let go of what stands in the way, you can't put anything new in its place. If your closet is full, you can't put in any new clothes. Or if you've got a boulder on your property, you have to remove it before you plant your garden. While many teachings tell you to let go of negative thoughts and beliefs, they don't give you a technology that tells you how. Now you'll have one.

Following is a simple, effective tapping technique I developed, based on Emotional Freedom Techniques (EFT). It comes from my book, *Vibrational Harmony,* and is an energy psychology technique. Energy psychology is sometimes referred to as acupuncture for the mind because you repeat certain statements, as you tap on acupuncture points.

The technique is very versatile and can be adapted to many issues and challenges. Of course we now will be using it to release whatever interferes with your diet and weight loss goals. The Releasing Category consists of both identification and releasing.

Identification – discovering the negatives

The first thing you need to do is identify your negative self sabotaging behaviors, and the negative statements you hear in your head and the negative images you see in your mind, related to your diet, your weight issues and how you feel about yourself.

Please be patient with yourself doing this exercise. It requires you to look deeply within. If you are honest with yourself, you will probably hear many insulting, derogatory comments and see many unpleasant, ugly images. It is vital to bring these to the surface so you can release them. They are keeping you from your goals as surely as if they were barbed wired fences.

Here are examples of the kind of statements you may hear in your mind: *"You're fat, and you'll always be fat. Who are you kidding, you'll never lose weight. I can't live without dessert every night. My mother always joked about my being an adorable pudgy baby. I hate going on an-*

other diet. I am going to fail again and I can't stand another failure. My husband (or wife) sabotages me by bringing home goodies I can't resist. Eating is my only pleasure. I have no will power. I can't do this. I'm too uncomfortable to exercise. I'm embarrassed to put on exercise clothes. I hate myself. It makes me so sad that I'm not able to control myself." Your statements may be worse than these, and some may surprise you. Keep going, and allow the statements and emotions to come up.

You may see images of yourself struggling to get into a seat in a plane, or being the overweight kid that everyone made fun of, or having your mom take away your candy at Halloween while all the other kids ate theirs. The statements you hear and the images you see come from your subconscious programs. Some of them are quite dreadful, so you want to delete them.

Technique for releasing negatives

After I explain the entire technique, I'll give you examples of how to create effective release statements. First, here's the formula statement for releasing the negatives you identify.

"Even though *(your release statement fits in here)*, I deeply and profoundly love, forgive and accept myself."

The reason you forgive yourself is because when human beings are unhappy with themselves they are in a powerfully negative state of self-condemnation and judgment. When you forgive yourself, it makes it easier for your subconscious to stop resisting and allow you to release negatives. However, if the word forgive is an issue for you, leave it out.

While you say the words, you'll tap lightly with two or three fingers on the points described on the next page. Say them out loud or to yourself. Don't just think them, say them.

Before you begin tapping, you'll take three deep breaths and take one breath after tapping on each of the points. Breathing in through your nose and out through your mouth is preferable, but is not essential.

You'll end the process with a deep breath and say, *Thank you.* You are giving gratitude to yourself, the Creator and/or the universe.

The tapping points

Point One: the fleshy part of your hand between the end of your little finger and wrist, the part of the hand that would be used to break bricks in Karate

Point Two: at the beginning of each eyebrow and directly above your nose, one finger touching the beginning of each eyebrow and middle finger at the point above your nose that is sometimes called the third eye

Point Three: on the bone at the outer corner of eye, one or both

Point Four: on top of your cheekbone, about one inch below the center of your eye, one or both sides

Point Five: indentation under your nose and above lips

Point Six: immediately below prominent knob on both collar bones simultaneously

Point Seven: on the inside of your wrist, one or both

Tap with your fingers flat, across entire wrist

Point Eight: on the top of your head, the crown

I recommend that you drink at least eight to ten glasses of pure water, to assist the releasing process. This is recommended for weight loss. Though many people don't do this and still benefit from releasing, it's a wise health practice. Your body is about 75% - 85% water, and drinking pure water helps you detoxify, whether the toxins are the result of junk food, environmental poisons or negative thoughts and emotions.

Creating release statements

To create your release statements, take a statement that you hear in your head. Let's use "You're fat, and you'll always be fat", as an example.

To fit this into the formula statement, which is: "Even though (your release statement fit in here), I deeply and profoundly love, forgive and accept myself," you'll say: *"Even though I have a program or belief that says you're fat and you'll always be fat, I deeply and profoundly love, forgive and accept myself."*

Repeat the statement three times while continuously gently tapping on your Karate Chop point.

You may also hear the statement as: "I'm fat and I'll always be fat." If so, as you tap on your Karate Chop point, repeat three times: *"Even though I have a program or belief that says I'm fat and I'll always be fat, I deeply and profoundly love, forgive and accept myself."*

You can release the statement both ways. Or you may have originally heard your mother say this. In that case, your statement is: *"Even though my mother told me I'm fat and I'll always be fat, I deeply and profoundly love, forgive and accept myself."*

When you tap on points two through eight, you say only the phrase that would be in parenthesis, once at each point. That phrase is: *I have a program that says I'm fat and I'll always be fat.* When you tap on these points, begin with the word, release. You can also leave out, I have.

Here's what you'll say as you tap on points two through eight: *"Release program that says I'm fat and I'll always be fat."*

Let's create a few more release statements. To release "I have no will power," gently tap on your Karate Chop point while repeating the following three times. *"Even though I have a belief (or program) that I have no will power, I deeply and profoundly love, forgive and accept myself."*

At points two through eight say: *"Release belief (or program) that I have no will power."*

Here's an example of how to release emotions. Let's use "It makes me so sad that I'm not able to control myself." The statement you repeat three times as you tap your Karate Chop point is: *"Even though,*

*it makes me so sad that I'm not able to control myself, I deeply and pro-
foundly love, forgive and accept myself."*

At points two through eight, say: *"Release my sadness at not being
able to control myself."*

Here's how to release an image. We'll use being the overweight
kid that everyone made fun of. While tapping on your Karate Chop
Point repeat three times: *"Even though I was the overweight kid that
everyone made fun of, I deeply and profoundly love, forgive and accept
myself."*

At points two through eight, say: *"Release image of myself as the
overweight kid that everyone made fun of."* I think you've got the idea
now. Have fun with it.

Concentrate on what you say and do with strong intention, and
expect positive results. As you tap, you may notice subtle changes,
such as tingling sensations, lightness, a relaxed or happier feeling, or
you may notice nothing. Something is happening, something good.

If you release daily you will be amazed at how effective it is. The
process peels away layers of negative energy from your nervous system and body, and also helps impress your subconscious that you no
longer want these old programs running your life.

Installing new programs

You install new programs through mental imagery and affirmations.
They are sometimes called intention statements or choice statements.

You may have used mental imagery and affirmations in the past
and found they didn't work. They don't because your subconscious is
filled with opposing images and statements. That's why we do releasing first.

And that's why I recommend that you do several releasing sessions with yourself, bringing to your awareness, and releasing as
many negative statements as possible before you begin installing

new programs. Don't be concerned whether you'll discover them or not; your mind tells them to you all the time. You want to release a good portion of negative programming, because, as the biblical statement says, *"You can't put new wine into old bottles."* Obviously, we're not talking about wine and bottles. The statement means you can't put new programs into a container, in this case, your subconscious mind that's already full.

Mental imagery: Imagining yourself with the body you desire, taking the appropriate action steps, imagine yourself in the clothes you want to wear, imagine yourself eating healthy foods, exercising, etc. Notice that I call this mental imagery and not visualization. Don't worry if you don't have a clear visual; many people don't. As long as you have a sense of yourself with the body you want and taking the action steps that can produce it, that's fine.

Affirmations: Speaking and hearing statements that you want to be true about your body and your behaviors. To make your affirmations more powerful and effective, tap on the same points that you used to release your old negative statements.

How do you tap in your affirmations? Simply say them once as you tap repeatedly on each point. Let's suppose that one of your affirmations is: I enjoy doing what it takes to have the body that pleases me. Say the complete statement one time as you continue tapping on Point One. Then repeat the statement, while tapping on Points Two through Eight.

Below I suggest some statements. However, your affirmations should be statements that feel and sound right to you. Try different ones until you find those that you feel you have the most resonance with. You will know they are right because you will feel enthusiastic and motivated as you say them.

· *I love myself and I love my body*
· *I am motivated to stay on my exciting new program*
· *I enjoy eating healthy foods that help me become slimmer*

· *I love looking in the mirror and seeing my smaller body*
· *I love going to the gym*
· *I love exercising, dancing, swimming, running, yoga –*
  whatever exercise you do
· *I love knowing that I will soon be wearing clothes in a smaller size*
· *I love hearing people admire me and my slimmer body*
· *I know that everything I am doing to take care of my body*
  is working for me
· *I am so pleased with myself for the success I'm having*
· *I enjoy my new healthy life-style*

Again, make up your own affirmations. I purposely avoided using the words "losing weight" because some people have very negative feelings when they hear those words. Other people have a belief
that the subconscious doesn't want to lose anything, so, to them, this
would not be a positive statement. Nevertheless, if those words feel
right to you, you can certainly say *"I'm delighted that I'm losing weight*
and keeping it off."

Integration: If you are concerned about integrating this into
your life, it's simple. When you do what Linda is lovingly teaching
you in this excellent book, and you continue to take care of your
mind by releasing as needed the negative self-talk statements, creating positive mental images, speaking and tapping on your affirmations and playing subliminal programs, you are integrating the new
programming into your life. For more information regarding EFT
and subliminal tapes, please refer to the Appendix.

Remember, the work you do on the conscious level is only successful when your subconscious mind is in agreement. This is true,
not just for weight issues, but for everything in your life.

Ending this section on healing techniques, we have learned, we
are all programmed. This concept is shared by therapists, healers and
people of the cloth. Again, these beliefs, programs, and thought pat-

terns are hidden in the unconscious mind, and they rule us and drive us to places we don't want to go.

It is likely that at least some of this information is new to you. Go gently. You now have wonderful information to draw upon daily in your life. You rock. Feel the possibilities.

Food is not your problem.

Diet programs, all with their special foods, counting calories, and fitness programs, don't mention any of the information contained here.

These **SECRETS** *are your answers.* This is a total program for transformation, change, happiness, and living the life you desire.

What could be next? The best is yet to come.

REMEMBER

*   Healing modalities are available
*   Relationships can trigger food issues
*   Heal the hurts that run you
*   Food can cover sexual and emotional abuse
*   What is eating us?
*   What we focus on we get
*   Reprogram your subconscious mind

PART V

THE SPIRITUAL

The kingdom of heaven is within you

♥

CHAPTER 17

The Kingdom of Heaven is Within You

SECRET. *YOU AND THE UNIVERSE are one, you are a co-creator.* How could you be any less than Divine? Remember, you have free will, the ability to choose. Your desires have been planted inside you to be fulfilled. You have the Power to make your dreams come true. Right now. Your dreams are calling you and wanting to be fulfilled.

So here we are. We have arrived at the door of Part V, the Spiritual. This is really the beginning of It. What do I mean by It? It is the magic where all the answers lie, the real YOU is inside you even as you read this.

We are taught in this society that something *out there*, something we can acquire, is the answer we seek. Many of us think: if only I could find that thing out there I would be happy. Or, more likely for those of us with eating issues, if only I could stop eating compulsively, if only I could be slim, if only. Then I could work on happiness, finding my career, finding my true love, money. Do you have an if only?

Some of us believe that in order to be spiritual we have to be poor. We have learned it all wrong. What if we've been coming at this from the wrong place? What if we already have it all inside?

I've learned that life is always lived from the inside out, not from the outside in; you are now unlearning the wisdom of the world. So far in this book you have learned many new skills, tools, and healing modalities to take with you on your new road, and your life is now filled with love, joy, gratitude and appreciation, daily. More and more peace and freedom await you. It's time to move into those emotions, free of angst about food, and peaceful about your choices. At times it won't be easy; the road will get bumpy and curvy. You may go though experiences which you would prefer to avoid but sometimes life happens. But unlike before, you will not be eating to avoid them, or as a way to distract yourself from them.

When life presents me with difficult circumstances these days, I forget to eat. In fact, food is the last thing I think of. That would have never happened when I was in the throes of compulsive overeating. And it might take some time, but if you keep working, keep asking, keep looking, food will no longer have power over you. Doesn't that thought feel great? Remember to feel the feeling many times during the day, and hold on to it. That is heaven on earth, and that is becoming your experience. You are changing and will continue to change without being aware of it. Like me, as time goes by, you will look back and ask, "Who was that person?"

I've mentioned how we are both the problem and the solution, for within us lies our healing. You have already begun to tap into it. What lies ahead is truly magical and a mystery; each of you will have your own experience of awakening. Re-discovering who you are is a delicious experience. **SECRET.** *Within YOU lie all the answers. It is a matter of learning how to access the truth, all the good that is inside.* Many powerful and easy Spiritual Practices are in this section and presented easily for you to follow.

In other words, the answer to food issues is ultimately Spiritual. **SECRET.** *The answer to any problem is spiritual; that I found out as I began to heal.* I know a power greater than I is at work in all areas of my life. When I forget that, I'm given a gentle or not so gentle reminder: I begin to obsess, trying to control the outcome of whatever is happening at that moment. When nothing I try actually works, I realize that I have taken charge again and not to my benefit. I have reverted back into my old ways: trying to do it all my way, pushing, pulling, stumbling, tripping, and feeling frazzled. When I feel that level of difficulty, that is a sign to step back and remember to trust in a power greater than I, who knows what is best for me. It is time for me to get out of the way. We are all powerful.

When we deal with the invisible and abstract, this move to trust takes a big leap of faith. **SECRET.** *Faith is like a muscle: it has to be worked to become stronger.* When we trust, things work out greater than we ever could imagine. I could share with you many experiences that I had that were disappointing at the time. Later I experienced something much greater than I could have ever dreamed of. It was a blessing I didn't get what I asked for. I'm sure you've had events in your life that worked out better than what you originally desired. True?

You also will get off track since that is part of the process but you will no longer run to food as a crutch. Life is giving you a sense of wholeness, and your foundation is becoming solid. New habits are forming that you don't have to think about and all your old, outdated habits are beginning to fade into nothingness. Now you can look to the future knowing your spiritual life will hold everything in place and at the same time give you more freedom than you could ever have thought possible. **SECRET.** *Life and living get better and better as each day unfolds.*

REMEMBER

* You are a co-creator
* The answer to any problem is Spiritual
* Exercise your faith muscle
* Life gets better and better

CHAPTER 18

Spirituality and Religion

❤

I'VE NEVER CONSIDERED MYSELF RELIGIOUS. Though I attended church as a child with my parents, we weren't religious in our home and I think for my parents church was just the thing to do with children. Spirituality though is a different story.

My father and I often took long walks in the woods; we walked in silence but I felt a power beneath my feet. I questioned the forest the same way I'd questioned the heartbeat I had felt resonating through my body the first time I became conscious of It. How did the trees get there, and what was I feeling when I walked under all the green umbrellas? The earth was throbbing, the same throbbing I felt when my heart was beating. It was this thing called Life. I knew I was connected to all that I felt and all that I saw.

In the winter, the trees were bare, and in the spring the beautiful buds decorated the branches. Autumn, the leaves fell in golden swathes and I saw early on the cycles of life. I learned to trust that things were happening in the invisible realm where I could only see the results, the buds, the golden leaves. The forest spoke to me in a silent language and I was captivated by the magnificence of It all. Who or what was behind the silence?

I'm deeply grateful that I attended regularly the great church under the sky with my father. It taught me at an early age that I was a part of something larger than myself. I felt It then and feel It now, and perhaps you also even though you may not be able to express it. Magic is going on in you. You know, deep in your soul. At this very moment, as your eyes are flowing across this page, your heart is beating, perhaps you are listening to music, perhaps a baby is developing in your womb. Whatever is happening, your body is playing a symphony of silent music and your Silent Partner is the conductor. The big YOU lives in the little you, and that is where you will find It. **SECRET.** *This is where healing begins and we continue to evolve Spiritually.*

I never knew I could use this thing called life to help me in any way or to overcome my problem with food but it happened. Perhaps you've chosen a name: Magic, Higher Power, Lord, Source, Spirit, God, Divine Intelligence, Energy, Presence. It is both the foundation and the spring from which all else comes. I suggest you choose a name. Any name will do and you may change the name from time to time. It does not know the difference, nor care.

REMEMBER

*   The big YOU lives inside
*   Your body plays a symphony

CHAPTER 19

Finding Magic in the Oddest Places

SECRET. *The concept of a power greater than I is the most important part of this program.* I'm not getting churchy on you and not suggesting you need to be in church or need to read the holy books. If you want to do that it is fine, but the key is the Spiritual aspect, not the specifics of which brand of Spirituality you choose. When you begin to live from a Spiritual space, all things are possible, and the possibilities are unlimited. You'll learn to trust this.

We all have our own paths to travel. We are always creating our lives, and now you are learning to be a deliberate creator, choosing what you desire to experience. Dig deep. The magic has been with you all your life, and you will have had moments like those I reveal.

Here is another memory, another moment of magic. It was over thirty five years ago. I was married at the time, unhappily, and deeply in the throes of compulsive overeating. The man I was married to was a very good man. I was the lunatic. I believed that it was someone else's responsibility to make me happy. Today's word is co-dependent. It was one of the lowest points of my life. We were traveling from New Jersey to Virginia and stopped in the Blue Ridge Mountains on Skyline Drive, a glorious scenic road with grand lookouts and areas along the way. Every view becomes more spectacular than the previous. We stopped at one of the rest areas and my husband went one direction while I went another. From the pavement, I stepped over the small barricade and walked about fifty feet into a meadow surrounded by trees, mostly pine, which perfumed the area. I felt a chill. It was the tail end of winter and I felt more alone than I had felt in a long time. No activity, no animals. Nothing but me, the sky, the pine trees, the gentle breeze, and the ground. I sat down, closed my eyes, and said this prayer: "God, if you are really there when I open my eyes I want to see a deer." I opened my eyes, pretty much expecting not to see a deer, and there in front of me, not ten feet away, were five of them. I sat in shock for awhile watching them graze, they watched me, and the deer and I became one. Everything was in perfect order in the Universe. I don't think this proves the existence of God. I do think it proves that there's more out there than just little me. A Power greater.

I have told that story only a few times throughout the years; now I am telling it in a grand way. Perhaps it was part of the plan because now I can suggest to "Ask, and it will be given." You will be heard. It might take a while, but you will be heard. Trust.

As I write I remember another magical moment. I was living in New York City and had just begun practicing Hatha Yoga. I was alone in my apartment one afternoon, had done the Yoga postures and breathing exercises and sat quietly. I was extremely relaxed and then, seemingly effortlessly, I realized I was more than my body, as if my body were a cover for something greater than the little me. I could not put the feeling into words. It was a space of silence and perfection. I knew who I was and where I came from, that oneness that is all there is. You have It. We are It. And we find this magic in the oddest places. Yet more was ready to unfold.

REMEMBER

* Live from a Spiritual space
* We create our lives
* We are more than our bodies

CHAPTER 20

A 12-Step Program Can Change Your Life

❦

I EVENTUALLY MADE MY WAY into a 12 step program. After resisting for a long time, I found myself at St. Cecelia's Church on 33rd Street in Manhattan, New York City, and immediately felt at home, finally, for the first time in my life. I remember sitting there saying to myself I'm going to get better. One after the other, the light bulb moments keep coming. I heard stories, similar to mine. People actually were doing the same insane things I was doing over food. I fit right in. People spoke with honesty about their behavior, what they were like before the program and what they were like after experiencing some recovery. I was inspired, hopeful, and encouraged, and I wondered why it had taken so long to get help. Everyone in 12 step programs hopes for a Spiritual experience. It is never clear when or how it will arrive but it will come into your heart if you truly desire to heal. Whatever form it takes, it's a life altering event. You will become brand new, see with new eyes, hear with new ears, zoom forward into another dimension. And don't be disappointed if it doesn't take the form you have expected, we all experience awakenings differently.

My spiritual awakening
It was early in the program when I had my Spiritual awakening. May 1977, shortly after my first meeting at St. Cecelia's in NY. I was living alone but not feeling alone, unusual for me. One afternoon I

had just finished eating lunch and I sat staring at the brown panel of wood in front of me. I felt content and peaceful. Time stopped and out of nowhere I felt a presence behind me. No one touched me, no one was there, no one physical. But something, some presence, was. I sat immobile, still as a pitch black night. And then it happened, in a flash, in an eternity. All the years of insanity, of running like the energized bunny, were lifted off my shoulders. Gone. Without a drum roll or call to attention. Instantaneous healing. The heavy cloud of negativity that walked every step with me found an escape hatch and vanished like magic.

And my obsession with food was gone. It was and continues to be the greatest gift in my life, besides my life. Where did it all go? Gone, out of nowhere, into nowhere. God? Magic? By whatever name, it was an awakening, the beginning of the journey on many levels. The end of one cycle and the start toward another place. I wasn't cured, but I was on my way, and would soon begin to understand that under my imperfections were more imperfections, layered with core issues, judgments about myself and everyone else, patterns, beliefs that I made up. It would take me some years to put those pieces together. What I know today is that under all those misconceptions are also brilliance, magnificence, perfection and mystery. **SECRET.** *Growing personally and Spiritually is like mining for gold.* You have to go through many layers to get to the essence, the purity and goodness of the deeper part of ourselves. As Deepak Chopra says, growing is like peeling away the onion skin. Today, I'm still uncovering the layers. It's painful at times but I move forward without obsessing over food.

I was unaware of my need for control, my ritualistic behavior, my rigidness around food, until I took a look at my behavior and actions when food was no longer a problem. Once I felt comfortable around food and didn't count calories or serving sizes, didn't weigh myself daily or hourly, I knew that my life was going to be perfect, finally. I was wrong. That was the beginning. From the Physical, I was led into the Mental, Emotional and Spiritual areas, and now for you, my path in revealing what has worked for me in my healing process.

I highly suggest finding a 12 step meeting in your area. Attend several meetings to find which one feels right for you. By attending the program and using the skills and techniques offered to you in **Lighten Up,** you will be on your way to becoming a brand new you.

In that moment of instant eternity, I was headed for a foreign land where the path was uncertain and the destination endless. I had no choice; it was my time. Your time is now and you can't turn back. **SECRET.** *And while your journey will be different than mine, we are all headed for the same destination.* Home.

That brings up a point: you're on your way now, but you will never get there, wherever there is, because life is eternal and your life and your healing are ongoing. You never get it all done, and that is the best part. There is always something new and wonderful to learn and to do. And challenges come from all arenas and areas.

Did my journey begin when I took my first breath or was it the first compulsive bite? Was it after my awakening, or did it begin years later? The answer is yes, all of it is part of the journey. **SECRET.** *We are all where we are at the present moment because of all our yesterdays.* One month, one year, five years from now we will all be very different individuals, and we will have a greater and deeper understanding of ourselves, of life and of how life works.

After the spiritual awakening

I kept attending meetings after my awakening. They were good, but I wanted to know more. I wanted to be in touch with something and I wasn't sure what that something was or where I would find it. I yearned to feel connected to something and I was not sure what that meant either. So I began the search. Living in New York City, I had at my disposal unlimited avenues to explore the arts, many places to explore new ideas, and all kinds of subject matter to investigate. I was looking for answers and I knew I would find them "out there", maybe in some form I never expected. I opened up to all possibilities.

My first experience with something out of the ordinary was with an interesting woman, Florence Meschner, who lived in the Bronx. She was a graphologist, a person who read the lines on your hands. Graphology is actually a studied science and takes years to become proficient. Please stay with me as it gets very interesting. I heard about her from a friend who had been ill. The doctors didn't know the nature of my friend's illness and someone recommended that she visit with Florence. Florence, by looking at the specific lines on certain points on my friend's hands, was able to pinpoint her physical condition. My friend told her doctor, the issue was confirmed, and she had an operation that saved her life. True story.

I wondered if Florence would have answers for me. I gathered my courage and armed with my image of her, a woman in a long flowing dress, dark hair, wearing a babushka, sitting in front of a crystal ball, I got on the subway from Manhattan to the Bronx. I rang her bell and the door opened to reveal Florence, a petite, white haired woman nothing like I'd imagined. She welcomed me into her home and I felt comfortable immediately. There was no crystal ball in sight. I looked.

She told me about my parents, my desires, my nature, talents and gifts, flaws, what I was good in, and things I had to address in order to heal and grow. She told me I would have to learn to say, "so what" to things in life that were unimportant and had no meaning. I was amazed how she knew me; I learned a lot about myself and saved the notes I took. I only went once, but it changed my life, and continues to change me. Occasionally, I look at them to see how the information fits into the present moment. It fits, all of it, no matter what's happening in my life.

It was during this same time period that I was introduced to the Science of Mind Philosophy, through a wonderful man named Carl Hubner. Carl was in his eighties and from the moment I met him, I felt I was in the presence of an enlightened soul. He seemed ageless, his eyes sparkled with life, kindness oozed from his being, and I connected with him on a deep soul level. We had many discussions about Life and living, and at one point he presented me with a great gift, a Science of Mind magazine. I was captivated and I knew that this philosophy could teach me what Carl knew. I immediately began attending the Science of Mind noon lectures on West 56th street in New York City, and attended their Sunday services at Lincoln Center regularly.

In the following years, I explored other philosophies, attended different churches and read many self help books. I investigated many alternative healing modalities. They were fascinating and seemed to have some truth, but I always came back to the Science of Mind, which teaches we don't have to go anywhere "out there" to find any answers: we are the answers, we are. It took me a long time to grasp that concept and I'm still learning every day.

I moved away from New York, traveled to Japan where I danced professionally for almost a year. I worked my way back to the states and found myself in Houston, Texas where I began taking classes at the Esoteric Center; classes were offered in astrology, numerology and tarot. I was fascinated with so many new ideas to consider, one of which was past lives. William David was an instructor who did Past Life Readings so I asked him to do one for me. Details are unnecessary. Suffice is to say that he told me I had been around a darn long time. Had I really lived all those lives? Was I really bringing some of my talents into this one? Did I sit under the olive trees in Egypt as a healer, a slave, in chains, in the galley of a boat? In a past life, did one of my brothers and I have conflicts that we were unable to resolve? Did we bring them forward into this life time? Had I really been a famous dancer in Spain? Had I been a Yogi who sat at the feet of Patanjali as a student? Was I bringing my past into the present? Was it true I had lessons to work out and people to settle issues with this go around? Were we here to work out our past? Could this be a stop over for a short period of time to gather more information so we could continue our journey in the invisible realm then come back again? Once we learned all that we could on this plain of existence, would we continue on to another dimension? I don't know but I certainly could relate.

The questions are endless, the answers indefinite. Ultimately, I enjoyed the readings, however; none of them gave me the feeling of being connected to myself or my Silent Partner. What I do know is that according to William, I have lived many lives. Perhaps I have and perhaps not. Perhaps you have also. Who knows? Or do we know deep down?

I know you all have your own stories to share, some more fanciful than this, some more grounded. I reveal these in order to make a point: through all this searching, the most important thing I learned was that I was always looking outside myself for the answers. I was running here and there, waiting for someone to tell me what to do and when to do it. To tell me how to live. I was running from myself, trying to find myself, and I was looking *out there* for me, for intimacy, for answers, for connection. Love and marriage are certainly one type of connection, but the deep connection I sought was not with another person, it was more. So I kept searching. And now?

I'm not an enlightened being, a Master or Guru. I'm very young in my development. But, I have peace and freedom around food issues, I know what worked. This is the reason for the book. I might not have the answers to many questions, but what I know is I'd like very much to help others along their paths.

CHAPTER 21

"Why Me, Why You"

MANY OF US ASK why we are faced with so many challenges. Why us? I believe that healing from these challenges allows us to help others and live from a higher level of consciousness. As the anonymous prayer from 12-step programs says:

Into your weak and feeble hands I have entrusted a Power beyond estimate. To you has been given that which has been denied the most learned of your fellows. Not to scientists or statesman, not to wives or mothers, not even to My spiritual leaders have I given this gift of healing other overeaters, which I entrust to you. It must be used unselfishly. It carries with it grave responsibility. No day can be too long, no demands upon your time can be too urgent, no case too pitiable, no task too hard, no effort too great. It must be used with tolerance, for I have restricted its application to no race, no creed and no denomination. Personal criticism you must expect, lack of appreciation will be common, ridicule will be your lot, your motives will be misjudged. Success will not always attend your efforts in your work with other overeaters. You must be prepared for adversity, for what men call adversity is the ladder you must use to ascend the rung toward spiritual perfection. I shall not exact of you beyond your capabilities.

You are not selected because of exceptional talents; and be careful always, if success attends your efforts, not to ascribe to personal superiority, that to which you can lay claim only by virtue of My gift. If I had wanted learned men to accomplish this mission, the power would have been entrusted to the physician and scientist. If I had wanted eloquent men, there would have been many anxious for the assignment, for talk is the easiest used of all talents with which I have endowed mankind. If I had wanted scholarly men, the world if filled with better qualified than you who would have been available. You were selected because you have an understanding heart, for your long experience as a compulsive overeater has made, or should make you, humbly alert to the cries of distress that come from the lonely hearts of overeaters everywhere. Keep ever in mind the admission that you are powerless, and that it was only with your willingness to turn your life and will into My keeping that relief came to you.

Think not that because you have abstained one day or one week, or one year, that it is the result of your unaided efforts. The help which has been keeping you normal will keep you so just as long as you live and follow what I have mapped our for you.

Beware of the pride that comes from growth, the power of numbers and invidious comparisons between yourselves of your groups whose success depends on numbers, money and position. These material things are not part of your creed. The success of material organization comes from the pooling of joint assets, yours from the union of mutual liabilities. Appeal for membership in material organizations is based upon a boastful recital of their accomplishments; yours on the humble admissions of weakness; the motto of successful commercial enterprise is: "He profits most who serves best," yours: "He serves best who sees no profit. The wealth of material organization, when they take their inventory is measured by what they have left; yours, when you take moral inventory." Anonymous

I believe I was chosen to show others my path, and show them the possibilities of following their own. **SECRETS** in the Physical, Mental, and Emotional Sections laid out the tools and techniques I have been using for over thirty years. You will respond in your own way, and find your truth, your path. You will close the book soon and the new you will continue to evolve, onward and upward on the spiral of endless moments and infinite possibilities.

I know you to be a magnificent creative being. I know there is no one like you. You are an exquisite expression of creativity. As each snowflake is unique and one of a kind, as each blade of grass in one of a kind never to be duplicated, so are you. You are as great as anyone or anything could ever be. This greatness is in You. It is YOU. There exists one Life, one Spirit, and It has many names all meaning oneness, wholeness, source, energy. Native Americans call it the Great Spirit, Lao Tzu calls it the Tao, traditional Christians say God. Even Einstein had his unified field theory. Some argue this is the same thing by a different name. You'll find It in a church, temple, mosque, tent, forest, and inside yourself. **SECRET.** *You will not find what you are looking for in others: husbands, wives, things, jobs, pills, or diets.* You will find it in you, and anywhere you stand can be a church, a temple, a mosque, a mountain, meadow: a Spiritual place.

Think in terms of health, wholeness and peace. Whatever we identify ourselves with, we become. What and who do you want to become? Claim perfection and experience radiant health wrapped in peace and joy, looking just the way you want, and feeling alive and energized.

REMEMBER

* A 12-step program can change lives
* We all have our time of awakening
* We are all headed home
* Life is eternal
* Find magnificence everywhere
* You've been gifted
* We are here to teach
* Think in terms of wholeness
* You are magnificent

CHAPTER 22

Turn Your Thoughts
to the Sacred

BLESSINGS, UPLIFTING QUOTES and affirmations follow, beautiful words from different philosophies and religions of the world to uplift your consciousness. We'll start with food, since that's what brought us together. I'm in the habit of always saying a blessing over my food. Be creative with your blessings.

Here are some of mine
· *Adjust this substance in such a way to meet the needs of all aspects of my total being leaving me healthy, happy, joyous and free.*
· *Thank you for my abstinence this day and freedom from compulsive overeating.*
· *Thank you for freeing me from all food issues.*
· *Bless this food and let it sustain my excellent radiant health in mind, body and spirit nourishing every part of my being.*
· *Thank you... Thank you... Thank you*

Uplifting quotes
Today I identify my body with the action of God, the radiant life of the divine being. Today I identify my physical body with my spiritual body, claiming that they are one and the same. Therefore I see that every organ, every action and every function of my body belongs to the rhythm of life, is a part of the radiant presence of the living spirit. There is one divine circulation flowing through everything, flowing through me right now.

There is one infinite rhythm at the center of everything. I am a part of this perfect whole. There is perfect circulation, perfect assimilation, perfect elimination. There is perfection in every part of my being, and wholeness and completeness. This physical body is a temple of the living spirit which animates it, sustains, it, rebuilds it, after the image of its own perfection, and keeps it in perfect health, in perfect harmony, in perfect wholeness.
Ernest Holmes, Founder of Science of Mind

Such beauty and wonder in those words, an elevated way of thinking, putting your focus on the sacred. **SECRET.** *Align yourself with perfection and the truth.* How great do you want your life to be? Super great.

From mystic Sufism
Drink from this heart now,
for all this loving it contains.
When you look for it again,
it will be dancing in the wind.
Shaikh Abu Saeed Abil Kheir - *"Nobody Son of Nobody"* -
Vraje Abramian

From Christianity
I am radiant with the health of God... then shall thy light break forth as the morning, and thine health shall spring forth speedily...
Isaiah 58:8

More from Ernest Holmes
I keep the promise. I shall keep the promise I have made to myself. I shall never again tell myself that I am poor, sick, weak, nor unhappy. I shall not lie to myself any more, but shall daily speak the truth to my inner Soul, telling it that It is wonderful and marvelous, that It is One with all of life, truth, power and action. I shall whisper these things into my Soul

until it breaks forth into songs of joy with the realization of Its limitless possibilities.
I shall assure my Soul.
Ernest Holmes

Our words are the activity of spirit within us.
Neglect not the gift that is in thee.
I Timothy 4:14

Beginning to understand the new you

You are removing the blinders from your eyes and the hurt and pain from your heart. Imagine looking at a beautiful picture on the wall and someone putting a filter between you and the picture. The picture remains the same but as soon as the filter is put in front of you, the picture becomes distorted. Now remove the filter and the picture is perfect. In the past, we lived with filters blocking our real selves.

You have no past, you are perfect. You are an open channel for thoughts that are positive, constructive, loving, and beautiful. What kind of a life will you live? What will your contributions be to the world, your passion?

SECRET. *There is no power in the past.* Food is your friend. You move through your days in joy, peace and happiness, eating what you want. Enjoy every morsel without guilt, pressure, fear or shame. It is your nature to be happy, joyous and free. Accept, accept, accept.

I imagine you don't know the dynamics of electricity, yet you know that when you flip a light switch, the light comes on. It turns off when you flip the switch again. Electricity is invisible, and it works whether we understand it or not. We know it works by the results.

Spiritual principles are invisible and we know they're working when we see and live the results. Take spiritual principles into your quiet time. Contemplate the golden thread that underlies religions and philosophies around the world: **SECRET.** *The golden thread: There is only one Power, one Source.*

Get ready for spiritual practices and breathing exercises to help calm your mind and body. The following will help you get to that place of peace and connectedness.

REMEMBER

*   You are blessed
*   Focus on the sacred
*   Spiritual principles are invisible
*   There is one Power in the Universe
*   Calm your mind and body

CHAPTER 23

Preparing for Your Spiritual Practices

♥

THE SPIRITUAL PART OFFERS you many spiritual practices that will lift your consciousness and expand your awareness of your Higher Self. As you change, everything changes. To begin to open up to the inner YOU, learn to be still in mind and body. One of the ways to do that is with your breathing; breathing exercises are simple and take minutes to practice, and are a natural tranquilizer to the body. Experience the exercises that follow and decide which you want to incorporate into your practice. Change them around. If you haven't downloaded my free audio on Mental Relaxation, please do so now at:

www.DietsDontWorkYouDo.com/relaxation.html

Breathing to calm the mind

You want to be in a quiet environment. Turn off the noise and go into a room by yourself. I've set up a small alter in one of my bedrooms with special pictures that make me feel loving, calm and peaceful. You can do something similar, or you can simply sit or lie on the floor. The important thing is to be physically comfortable, not hot or cold and wearing comfortable clothing. Wherever you end up, sit or lie with your back straight so the lungs will receive oxygen, be properly ventilated and not be collapsed. If you sit, think of having a string on the top of your head and someone is pulling it up. Your spine is straight and your body lifted.

If you are lying on the floor, place a small book on your stomach. If you prefer sitting, place your hands on your stomach. Instructions are to: breathe in through your nose, and exhale through your nose until all the air is completely out of your lungs. Now you are ready to begin. While lying down, inhale very slowly to the count of four, pushing the book toward the ceiling. If you are sitting, push your hands out. Very slowly exhale through your nose to four counts and feel your stomach move toward your spine. After you learn the exercise, remove the book and practice without your hands.

Breathe in four counts then breathe out four, pushing your stomach toward your spine. As you exhale, be aware of your body melting into the floor or chair, letting go of stress and tension. On the inhalation, silently say a positive statement, and on the exhalation release something you don't want. For example, "*I am energized throughout the day*" on the inhalation, and "*I let go of fear, doubt, worry, shame and guilt*" on the exhalation.

Do this in the morning before your day begins and at the end of the day for five to ten minutes. You'll feel the changes immediately.

The complete breath

This can be done lying on the floor or in bed, sitting on the floor or sitting in a chair. Again breathe in and out through your nose. Exhale all the air completely from the lungs, place your hands on your stomach and begin inhaling slowly four counts, pushing the stomach toward the ceiling. Continue breathing and gently place your right hand on the right side of your rib cage, your left hand on the left side of your rib cage, and count five and six. Feel the air expanding the rib cage area. On seven and eight, place your hands on your chest. Feel the air coming in and raising the chest area, bringing the air all the way up to the collar bone area. Remember to breathe smoothly without any gasping or holding your breath. Now you are ready to let go and relax into the floor. As you continue the smooth breathing, begin exhaling to the count of eight. Release the air from the chest and rib cage area, concentrating the last four counts on the stomach touching the spine. A good image to use is a wave as it flows up and moves back down.

These two breathing exercises are wonderful ways to relax your body, free your mind, and put you into the place of total relaxation.

Mental relaxation technque

Before you do anything, lie or sit for a moment and silently tell yourself this is your time to experience peace, relaxation and pleasure. In this exercise, you can be lying on the floor, lying in bed, or sitting with eyes closed. Again, the key is to be comfortable physically. If you are lying down, separate your feet about twelve inches apart, your arms about twelve inches away from the sides of your body, palms facing the ceiling, and close your eyes. If you are sitting, plant your feet on the floor, back straight against the chair, palms resting in your lap with one hand resting in the other or palms facing up on your thighs, and eyes closed. Do several rounds of the complete breath. Start silently with the following, and as you give yourself each command think it through, and feel your body melt into the floor or chair remembering to take your time, don't rush. Now you are ready to relax your body. Begin your commands by saying:

· *I send my mind to relax my right foot and all the toes on my right foot.*
· *I relax the outside of my right ankle, the inside of my right ankle.*
· *I relax the top of my foot, the bottom of my right foot, my heel.*
· *I send my mind to relax my right calf, right shin, right knee, right thigh, right hip and right buttock.*
· *I send my mind to relax my left foot and all the toes on the left foot.*
· *I relax the outside of my left ankle, the inside of my left ankle.*

· *I relax the top of my left foot, the bottom of my left foot, and my left heel.*
· *I send my mind to relax my left calf, left shin, left knee, left thigh, left hip and left buttock.*
· *I send my mind to relax my right hand and all the fingers on my right hand.*
· *I relax the top of my right hand, the palm of my right hand.*
· *I relax my wrist, lower arm, elbow, upper arm and my right shoulder.*
· *I send my mind to relax my left hand and all the fingers on my left hand.*
· *I relax the top of my left hand, the palm of my left hand.*
· *I relax my wrist, lower arm, elbow, upper arm and my left shoulder.*
· *I send my mind to relax my stomach, my intestines, my kidneys, liver, gall bladder, pancreas and spleen.*
· *I send my mind to relax my breasts, my lungs, the muscles around my heart…my heart is working perfectly well with all the other systems in my body.*
· *I send my mind to relax my tailbone, lower back, my middle back, my upper back, my shoulders.*
· *I relax the front, back and sides of my neck.*
· *I relax my lower jaw, upper jaw, lips, tongue, nose, right cheek, right ear, right eye, right eyelid.*
· *I relax my left cheek, left ear, left eye, left eyelid, forehead and scalp.*
· *I send my mind to the space between my eyes brows and relax totally.*
You may end here and stay in this space for a while for total relaxation.

REMEMBER

* As you change, everything changes
* Breathing is a natural tranquilizer
* Spend time to mentally relax your body

CHAPTER 24

Spiritual Practices

BY THE TIME YOU get to the head area, you may be asleep. If you are, that's fine. You needed the rest; however, do try to stay awake and be present in what you are doing. This space you experienced is called *centering* and is an excellent space to sit quietly and say your affirmations. You have reached the core of your being. You may choose to sit in silence. Silence is healing.

You may chose not to do the breathing exercise or the mental relaxation technique. Instead with eyes closed, go straight to the space between your eyebrows. Focus your attention on this space and you'll also be centering. You will have entered a quiet, inner room, a place of peace and tranquility. Your thoughts of food, or irrational behavior, your emotional turmoil may not be solved but it will recede in the face of you being centered.

When you're ready to come back, gently open and close your eyes a couple of times. Then slowly, if you're lying down, roll to one side and gently push with both hands to come up to a sitting position. Talk a moment and then stand up. If you've been sitting, open and close your eyes and when you're ready take your time in getting up. You're relaxed and ready for your next event in life.

Enjoy the following passages:
Sweet song of the Silence, forever singing in my heart.
Words cannot express, the tongue cannot tell:
Only the heart knows the songs
Which were never sung, the music

Which was never written.
I have heard that great Harmony and felt that great presence.
I have listened to the Silence; and in the deep places of Life, I have stood
naked and receptive to Thy songs and they have entered my soul.
I am lost in the mighty depths of Thy inner calm and peace.
Ernest Holmes

Beneath The Clamor of the World
You long for peace. You think of peace as being goodwill towards each
other, good will among the nations, the laying down of arms. But peace
is far more than this, it can only be understood and realized within your
heart. It lies beneath all the turmoil and noise and clamor of the world,
beneath feeling, beneath thought. It is found in the deep, deep silence and
stillness of the soul. It is spirit: it is God.
White Eagle

Contemplation is another powerful spiritual practice. The objective is to gain a deeper understanding of a topic of interest or an object. Choose something daily that lifts your spirits: a passage from the Bible, the Talmud, the Koran, or any sacred text. Or choose an uplifting paragraph or statement, or a walk in nature. Whatever you choose, simply contemplate it, think about it, experience it. Remember and think upon these thoughts throughout the day, and realize that we are all one, we are all a part of everything else. If anything is weighing you down, whether you are thin, overweight, or miserable trying to maintain, go to a quiet place and be still. Relax, meditate, contemplate. In that space there is nothing but goodness and peace, no fear, no guilt, no remorse, only love for you. **SECRET.** *Beyond all of our thoughts and feelings about our problems with food there is a place that knows no pain, misery, sadness or compulsion.* Here lies our power, strength and answers. Practice, practice, practice.

A lovely passage for contemplation

Be still and know that I am God. I am still in Thy Presence. I am quiet and peaceful, for I put my trust in Thee. A great stillness steals over me and a great calm quiets my whole being, as I realize Thy presence. The heart knows of Thee, O Most High within. It is still in Thy Presence, and it puts its whole confidence in Thee alone. In Thy presence I am still.
Ernest Holmes

Meditation has been practiced for centuries, in cultures worldwide. It is listening to the quiet voice inside.

Joel Goldsmith tells us *"Meditation is an invitation for God to speak to us, or to make Himself known to us; it is not an attempt to reach God, since God is omnipresent. The Presence already is. The Presence always is, in sickness or in health, in lack or in abundance, in sin or in purity; the Presence of God always and already is. SECRET. We are not seeking to reach God, but rather to achieve such a state of stillness that the awareness of God's presence permeates us"* (Goldsmith, 96). That is really the main function of meditation.

Meditation with your inner advisor

Here is a beautiful meditation that will lift your spirits. It is powerful and life affirming, bringing you much joy and a sense you are truly loved. It is an opportunity to resolve a problem or to gain knowledge or information. Information regarding food issues can be brought to the surface, which can be extremely valuable and healing. Whether you have a specific issue or dilemma in mind, or go into the meditation with the intention of having it revealed to you, this meditation is helpful. It offers a new way to approach any issue.

While sitting in a chair, calm your mind and body by doing a breathing exercise of your choice. Move easily into a quiet and still place within. Imagine a beautiful scene from your life's experience, or create it as you go, and don't be concerned if you can't imagine something specific. Make it a safe place, peaceful and serene.

Now, invite your Inner Adviser to join you in your tranquil setting. Your Inner Advisor is that voice inside you that always speaks truth and wisdom. You may not be used to hearing this voice, but it is there. It always was and always will be. You will sense its wisdom and desire to help you. Ask its name, and invite this Being to have a conversation. You will feel as if you are having a real conversation. Tell your Inner Advisor what is concerning you. Tell all. Ask your Inner Advisor what you need to know. Listen with your heart. This is an excellent time to converse about your weight issues. For example, what are the things that are holding you back? What is holding you from becoming brand new? What are the changes you need to make in your life in order to heal? The questions are endless and not only pertaining to weight issues. Just converse. It is important to take your time with this process.

Ask this Being what action you need to take to move in a direction in your life that would be empowering. Spend some time here, several minutes or more. I feel confident answers will come. If at first this special Being does not visit with you, don't become discouraged. Try again.

When you are ready, thank your Inner Advisor and say goodbye. Begin by feeling your feet on the floor. Feel your body in the chair. Slowly open and close your eyes several times and come back to the present moment. This is a perfect time to journal your experience and record your information. I know you will feel loved, supported and cared for. Know that it is safe for you to return at any time, and remember that there may be a different Being each visit. Let it happen. It will always be perfect.

How to give a spritual mind treatment, affirmative prayer

SECRET. *You don't have to go to church to pray. Pray in your car, in a mosque, a temple, a tent or on the beach.* Pray silently, out loud, alone or together. Choose your version of prayer, and just pray. Following are a number of ways to pray and yours may be different still.

Ernest Holmes, Founder of the Science of Mind Philosophy, developed a style of prayer called affirmative prayer also known as a Spiritual Mind Treatment. One of my dear teachers, Dr. Jesse Jennings, the Minister of Creative Life Spiritual Center in Spring, Texas, writes: "I don't believe one can treat too often, and the words don't especially matter except insofar as they do or do not stimulate feelings. We can treat or affirm till we're blue in the face, though nothing, or not very much will change until we feel the emotional impact of the truth we are declaring. Our Spiritual practice is about the whole self. All states of consciousness: our beliefs about money, work, friendship, our body and so forth are connected, and they ultimately come down to our basic belief that we are either inside or outside of life's meaning. In doing Spiritual Mind Treatment, we not only cause ourselves to cross paths with our preferred states of being, but we also learn who we really believe we are and why." (Quoted by permission from pamphlet titled "Speaking Your Word." The customary way to express a treatment is in five steps:

· *Recognition.* Recognize the existence and immanence of Spirit.

· *Identification.* Sometimes called unification. Identify yourself as an expression of Spirit.

· *Realization.* Realize that whatever state or condition you desire is likewise an expression of Spirit, and is thus right where you are.

· *Thanksgiving.* Allow yourself to feel grateful for this being so.

· *Release.* Release the total idea in order for it to become form.

Dr. Jennings continues, "If you take only the first two steps, you are meditating and communing with Spirit. The third step by itself is a simple affirmation. Put them all together, along with gratitude (which isn't so much a formal step as a natural reaction), and then let go, and you have a complete treatment. The intuition of the mind during this time in meditation can offer solutions that the rational mind can't.

Treatment is a movement in thought and feeling. It doesn't

change Spirit. Its central premise is that Spirit is all, and this is chiefly how treatment differs from petitionary, intercessory form of prayer that supposes a God who dwells somewhere else and who may respond capriciously, if at all.

Treatment works by redirecting feeling, yet it is about more than just feeling better while suffering unchanged conditions. It changes things. With the universe being a whole Spiritual System, everything you can imagine is already contained with it. Allow yourself spontaneity in your treatments. The whole point is to bring yourself to the place where you believe what you're saying. You may wish to combine steps, or add some of your own. Spirit will congeal around the word you've spoken.

Treatment is an affirmative, accepting prayer that recognizes that there is no ultimate reality to negative conditions or feelings. It is a period of communion with one's higher Self. Treatment is action, an act of profound faith in a Power greater than oneself, that's invisible to the eye. Because it is invisible we sometimes forget to trust it, but treatment is just as real as the sweat of our brow – more real, in truth, because it relates to the causes of things, not just their appearances. Remember, every form is just a congealed idea, and every idea can be changed by an act of consciousness".

A spiritual mind treatment for food and a healthy body

Reverend Martha Quintana is the minister of the Rio Grande Center for Spiritual Living in Albuquerque, New Mexico. She has offered this prayer especially for you. Say it with feeling and it will come to pass. This is the truth of your being.

"There is One Creator, One Life, One Higher Power behind all life. I call this One, Spirit, and Spirit is pure Creation. It is the Creator and the Created. It is the Alpha and the Omega – beginning and the end. It was, is, and always will be. Spirit is the pure pattern and perfection of Life. This Life is my Life now for I have not and cannot be separate from It. It

is who I am and It is all I am. I live in Spirit, and I, too, am the beginning and the end and I am eternal life. Spirit's pattern and perfection live in me and I am whole, perfect, and complete.

Any sense of separation is only an illusion. All that I have and all that I need is given to me at every step. I, too, am like the lilies of the valley and the birds in the air. All my needs are provided.

In this moment, all is well. I have a home, food, clothing, love, and self-esteem. Because of this, I am able to step into the World of the Spirit and know myself for the first time. I shift any ideas that stand between me and the sunlight of the Spirit. I am free to choose a different life right here, right now. I know I am not my body. I am pure spirit, free to choose.

I choose freedom. I am no longer a slave to food. Instead, I live freely. I eat foods that give my body health. I am eating foods that allow me to remember God's perfect pattern of goodness. I live in a healthy body at a healthy weight. I am free. I am loved. I am whole.

And I give thanks. I am grateful for good food and a healthy body. I am grateful that I have good relations with all people around me. Most of all, I am grateful that I love and I am loved. My life is a good life.

I surrender this prayer to the essence of Spirit with the knowledge that all is well. Amen."

THE·PRAYER·OF·THE·CHALICE

Father, to Thee I raise my whole being
~a vessel emptied of self. Accept, Lord,
this my emptiness and so fill me with
Thyself~Thy Light, Thy Love, Thy
Life~that these Thy precious Gifts
may radiate through me and over-
flow the chalice of my heart into
the hearts of all with whom I
come in contact this day
revealing into them
the beauty of
Thy Joy
and
Wholeness
and
the
serenity
of Thy Peace
which nothing can destroy~

Father, to Thee I raise my whole being ~a vessel emptied of self.
Accept Lord this my emptiness and so fill me with Thyself~ Thy Light~Thy Love~
Thy Life~that these Thy precious Gifts may radiate through me and over flow the
chalice of my heart into the hearts of all with whom I come in contact this day
revealing into them the beauty of Thy Joy and Wholeness and the serenity of Thy
Peace which nothing can destroy~. Anonymous

In essence, prayers come in many forms. By practicing these or your variation of spiritual practices, you will get a glimpse into the Truth of your being. **SECRET.** *The more you turn inwardly, the more you'll experience your food issues melting away.* These practices help you to realize the Unity of all Life.

REMEMBER

* Practice, Practice, Practice
* Breathing to calm the mind
* The complete breath
* Body-mind relaxation
* Centering
* Contemplation
* Meditation
* Affirmative prayer

CONCLUSION

The End, the Beginning

I SIT STARING at the blank page asking what words shall I write next. I feel I have so much more to share and yet nothing more. There are those contradictions again. I was given a gift, compulsive overeating, so I could reach out and find my happiness. I found my happiness by turning within and sharing many powerful **SECRETS**, *adding up to freedom in many areas of my life and I know yours also.*

You are one with It, the Universe, this Mystery, this Beauty. Could we ever begin to comprehend this mystery? Would we get very far? Perhaps there is no explanation. However, if we stop and look around, the miracles are before our eyes. Every blade of grass, the sun, the moon, the stars, the air we breathe, the food we eat to nourish our bodies come from this field of unlimited potentiality. Even puppy breath.

I know you are magnificent beyond your wildest imagination. You are gifted and possess talents that no one else has. You are capable of doing great things in your life and have the Power to create a life full of miracles. You are a miracle maker. Everything seen and unseen, known and unknown come from a place of purity, a place of perfection. You have come from this place of perfection. Everyone.

You are a co-creator and have come to create a life of happiness, peace and love, all the good you could ever imagine and more. You are now on the path discovering how to unlock your greatness. You are great. You are perfect, whole and complete.

It has been a joy and great honor to share these concepts, great **SECRETS,** and my recovery with you along with many tools, techniques, and healing modalities that have proven results. I am grateful for the information the other healers have contributed. I have enjoyed sharing the magic I experience daily. I know each person reading this book continues to be affected in the most positive ways as time unfolds, living happy, joyous and free.

You have made peace within your soul and with food issues, living an unprecedented life in gratitude and appreciation. Please share with others the many golden **SECRETS** in **Lighten Up**.

Your life is a gift and you are the gift to yourself and others. Call forth your special gifts and talents. You are here to make a difference. You are needed and are here by Divine Appointment. You are in my heart. We are One.

Please let's stay in touch. www.DietsDontWorkYouDo.com

You have everything you need to manifest your greatness. Let life have a great time with you.

Diets Don't Work YOU Do

YOU'RE FREE NOW

YOU ARE THE GREATEST GIFT OF ALL

Appendix A:
More Information on Sexual Abuse by Dell deBerardinis
Possible distorted beliefs of survivors

Sexual abuse as with other abuses dramatically affects a survivor's belief about herself and her relationship with the world. Here are some possible distorted beliefs that drive behavior and lifestyle:

· *I wanted the abuse, therefore I am bad.*
· *Telling the secret equals death.*
· *It is my responsibility to keep my family safe. I must sacrifice myself.*
· *I am bad to the core. The abuse happened because I deserved it.*
· *I must never let anyone know me, or they will find out how bad I am.*
· *I don't deserve anything good. I deserve to be punished.*
· *It's dangerous to speak up, show feelings, or ask for help.*
· *Love is supposed to hurt. Sex and love are the same.*
· *I have no power. I don't have the right to say no.*

Defensive responses to abuse

The trauma occurs resulting in overwhelming feelings. Victims create coping skills and defenses in order to protect themselves and survive. Defenses are used to avoid feelings and memories. Here are some typical defenses:

    A. Emotional Defenses:

      Shock
      Denial
      Isolation
      Justifying
      Dissociation
      Control

Minimizing

Rationalizing

Disassociating

B. Behavioral Defenses:

Increased risk taking/Acting out sexually

Rejecting others/Perfectionism

Suicidal Thoughts/Behaviors denying personal needs

Caretaking others/Chemical dependency

Anorexia/Bulimia

Overeating Sexual addiction

Compulsive shopping/Compulsive cleaning

Workaholism/Sleep disorders

Creating crises/Anger outbursts

Projection/Hyper vigilance

Lack of boundaries/Startle response

Inability to feel love/Denial of positive feelings

Eventually these defenses fail to keep memories and feelings from reaching consciousness and the victim begins to re-experience the trauma.

Specific issues in recovery

Some specific issues that I believe should be addressed in recovery are:

The child within. Meet the child within you! This can be done through a variety of techniques. A survivor can begin the journey back in time by writing an autobiography, gathering information from family members who are willing to share. Digging out old photos, visiting a toy store, or being around and observing young children the age the abuse occurred is helpful. Therapists often use techniques such as visual imagery, hypnosis, art and writing letters to the inner child to develop the relationship.

A plan for managing panic attacks and flashbacks. There needs to be a way to manage flashbacks and the scary times in recovery. Terror is the emotion associated with these states and can be overwhelming when it resurfaces. A survivor needs a support group or a list of individuals they can call when in a difficult situation. Techniques such as journaling, meditation, getting centered, deep breathing, etc. are also possibilities. Oddly enough flashbacks are opportunities to heal. They are a piece of the unfinished trauma coming into the conscious mind, not previously experienced, making it available for processing and letting go. Safety to experience these traumatic times is extremely important.

Relationship detachment. Relationships for survivors are often enmeshed, distanced, or abusive. I believe the very core of healing is about putting closure on the past relationships with family, the perpetrator, or others who no longer serve to meet the survivor's needs. I suggest techniques such as goodbye letters, empty chair dialogues, writing a divorce decree, etc. as ways to let go of past connections. It is essential to healing and to being present in current relationships. In order to do this work, survivors may need help to establish contractual arrangements or boundaries with current relationships (Example: sexual abstinence for a period of time). Because current relationships often reflect past abuse, they will experience transition and change as the survivor "grows through" past experiences.

Confrontation. Confrontation helps survivors take back their power from the perpetrators. I believe it first needs to be done within the safety of a counselor's office or with a trusted person around by role playing or using other methods of re-creating the meeting until the survivor is comfortable and has processed much of the terror and rage of the abuse.

Support system. The survivors must take responsibility for their recovery every step of the way. This includes asking for support. It is helpful if this support is from people who have themselves experienced similar problems. This can be found in 12-step groups or other group settings specific to survivors' needs. Learning to ask for help is a big step for survivors but critical to the healing process. No one heals from abuse all alone.

Forgiveness. There are many questions raised about forgiveness in relationship to the victimization of children and adults. My observation of my clients who had been abused is that forgiveness came as an end product to the process described above of grieving the losses, confrontation, and closing out abusive-relationships. As the survivor heals, the outside world looks different. AND as the survivor heals the process of self forgiveness takes place. It is impossible to forgive others if one has not adequately forgiven oneself.

Spirituality. Sexual abuse splits the self and often interferes with the individual's ability to connect to and believe in a Supreme Being. This belief may be interfered with in the traumatic event of the child's perception that he or she is profoundly alone. My belief is that this reconnection within the spiritual self is a necessary part of healing.

Use of the twelve-step programs in recovery

I have briefly mentioned the twelve step programs as an adjunct to treatment. The use of the steps for survivors of trauma works well in a number of ways. I have found that survivors who have been willing to engage in a 12-step program progressed much faster through the healing process. There are some very significant reasons for this. First, there is a very high correlation between the incidences of childhood sexual abuse, substance abuse and alcoholism. In cases of family abuse, there is a primary addictive process going on, possibly drugs or alcohol, eating disorders, or sexual addiction or religion. The addictive processes are often used by the survivor as well, as a primary coping skill. Some programs that are successfully treating sexual offenders are using a 12-step model developed by Patrick Carnes and based on the AA philosophy. The 12-step programs address many of the things related to the issues of sexual abuse such as powerlessness, unmanageability, denial, spirituality, and taking an inventory of the past. Find a group that works for you and stay with it.

Therapeutic techniques for use with survivors
Some other suggested techniques for recovery are:

A. **Written Therapies** such as journaling feelings and thoughts suggested that survivors keep an ongoing daily journal.

B. **Trance and Trance State Therapies** such as hypnotherapy, regression and guided imagery that help with memory retrieval. Dream reenactment or a dream journal is suggested. Dream reenactment can be done by writing or imaging the dream as if it is just now happening.

C. **EMDR.** (Eye movement desensitization and reprocessing) A bi-lateral technique that moves trauma out of the brain. It is highly effective and a rapid healing technique.

D. Expressive Therapies such as art, music, dance, story telling, psychodrama, and roleplaying are a way to release emotional trauma.

E. Gestalt techniques such as empty chair playing out the victim and the offender.

F. Rage reduction techniques using a plastic bat, a beanbag, or any safe tool. Rage work is necessary work for survivors and can also be done with EMDR.

D. Body Awareness Techniques such as breath therapy, massage, pressure point therapy and Rolfing help the body release the abuse.

Sexual abuse: a selected bibliography

· Alcoholics Anonymous World Services, Inc. New York City. 1976.

· American Psychiatric Association, Diagnostic and Statistical Manual of Mental Disorders (4th rev.). Washington, DC.

· Bass, Ellen and Davis, Laura. The Courage to Heal. NY: Harper & Row, 1988.

· Blume, Sue. Secret Survivors. New York: Ballantine Books, 1989.

· Booth, Leo. When God Becomes a Drug. Pompano Beach, FL: Health Communications, 1988.

· Braun, B. G. "The BASK Model of Dissociation," Part 1. Dissociation, 1 (1), 423.

· Carnes, Patrick. Out of the Shadows. Minneapolis, MN: Compcare, 1983.

· Forward, Susan. Toxic Parents. NY: Penguin Books, 1979.

· Kasl, Charlotte Davis, Ph.D. Women, Sex and Addiction. NY: Harper & Row, 1989.

Gratefully acknowledged for their contributions to
Lighten Up, Diets Don't Work, YOU Do!

Beverly Nadler
Saundra Dickinson
Dell deBeradinis
Bill Fergerson
Rev. Jesse Jennings
Rev. Martha Quintana

Holmes, Ernest, The Science of Mind The Thirty-Fifth
Edition (New York, NY: Dodd, Mead, & Company, 1938),
517.

Holmes, Ernest & Barker, Raymond Charles, 365 Days of
Richer Living (Los Angeles, CA: Science of Mind Publish-
ing, 2001), 73.

Sams, Jamie, "Earth Medicine," n.d., http://www.angelfire.
com/md/elanmichaels/naquotations.html, (November 1
2010).

White Eagle, The Quiet Mind (Fletcher and Son LTD
Norwich, England, 1972), 38

Covey, Stephen R., Principle-Centered Leadership (New
York, NY: Simon & Schuster,
1990, 1991), 49

Dyer, Wayne, You'll See It When You Believe It (New York,
NY: W. Morrow, 1989) 56

Isaiah 58:8   Old Testament

Timothy 4:14   New Testament

Goldsmith, Joel, Practicing the Presence (New York, NY: Harper, 1958) 96

Williamson, Marianne, A Return to Love (New York, NY: Harper-Collins, 1993) 120-121

Ferguson, Bill, private email correspondence. May 2006.

Nadler, Beverly, private correspondence. November 2010.

Quintana, Martha, private correspondence. November 2010.

deBerardinis, Dell, Therapy Made Simple, adapted for Diets Don't Work YOU Do, November 2010.

Information regarding Beverly Nadler, EFT and subliminal tapes:

Beverly Nadler
www.breakthroughhealth.net
www.vibrationalharmonybook.com

Excellent support for you:
SCWL subliminal audio programs (CD's and tapes) by Midwest Research, are wonderful support tools that can assist you in reprogramming your subconscious. View them at: www.bevrlynadler.com/order_scwl.html. SCWL stands for Subconscious to Conscious Without Limitations.

Several Weight Loss audios are available. If you have any questions about these superb re-programming tools, please contact Beverly. Contact information is on the site.

CPSIA information can be obtained at www.ICGtesting.com
Printed in the USA
LVOW011221090213

319419LV00002B/9/P